The Needlepoint Pattern Book

The NEEDLEPOINT

PATTERN BOOK

by Dennis M. Arnold

Photography by Rica Molofsky

WILLIAM MORROW & COMPANY, INC.
NEW YORK

1 2 3 4 5 78 77 76 75 74

Library of Congress Cataloging in Publication Data

Arnold, Dennis M
    The needlepoint pattern book.

    Bibliography: p.
    1. Canvas embroidery—Patterns. I. Molofsky,
Rica, illus. II. Title.
TT778.C3A76   746.4'4   73-22143
ISBN 0-688-00241-2

DESIGNED BY JACK JAGET

To Stephanie and all my family who encouraged me,
and especially to my father,
who would never have believed I finished it

ACKNOWLEDGMENTS

I would like to extend a special thanks to Narcisse Chamberlain for making a complex job easier; to Pam Hatch for her patience in reading through with me; to the contributors for the use of their designs; and to Rica Molofsky for so expertly photographing each piece of needlepoint.

CONTENTS

LIST OF COLOR PLATES

INTRODUCTION

Of recent years, needlepoint has become one of the most amazingly popular crafts in the country. Shops devoted exclusively to needlepoint abound, and "art needlework" in department stores now takes up large sales areas instead of the dusty corners it once did. Needlepoint kits and painted canvases are sold in styles, colors, and sizes for every purpose imaginable. But there is still one impediment: good needlepoint designs are expensive.

In THE NEEDLEPOINT PATTERN BOOK, I have collected over fifty designs by some of the best professionals in the United States and provided an easy-to-copy pattern for each one, so that you can stitch these original designs for a fraction of the cost of buying them in a shop. I have tried to vary the collection—giving you designs of different styles, projects for different purposes, and patterns from the simplest to the quite complex. There are purses, belts, pillows, wall hangings, pictures, children's toys, Christmas decorations. Some of the patterns are for the inexperienced (some are even appropriate for children to do), and others are for experienced needlepointers who want a challenge. Many of the designs easily allow for alteration and experimentation with the colors, sizes, stitches, borders, or any other aspects that you feel would suit you better done differently from the original.

However, great care has been taken to give you all the information you need to duplicate these designs exactly—if you want to—through accurate drawings of the patterns, with each area numbered for the color originally used by the designer (with further advice on choosing colors on page 22), and through the suggestions for working the designs that accompany each pattern.

Since the main purpose of this book is to provide professional designs for do-it-yourself needlepointers, only basic needlepoint techniques are covered in this introduction and they are set forth rather briefly, for the same information is available over and over again in many other books. In the Bibliography on page 183 is a list of some of the best of the many books in print that go into greater detail and can tell you anything you want to know about the fine points of needlepointing. The experts who buy THE NEEDLEPOINT PATTERN BOOK will not need the advice that follows, but since it is a book for beginners as well, the basics and a few of the pitfalls are described.

MATERIALS

If you are a beginner, you must first know about the materials of needlepoint—which aren't many: canvas, wools, needles, and scissors.

CANVAS

All needlepoint canvas has an "open" weave: you can see right through it. It comes in two basic types: mono (or single-mesh) canvas and penelope (or double-mesh) canvas.

Mono canvas is a comparatively modern innovation and convenient to work on. The mesh, or spacing, of the weave is formed by the crossing of single threads, and the canvas looks rather like window screening. Stitches are taken on it diagonally across each intersection of single threads. Mono canvas is made of white cotton and is stiffer than penelope. Some stitchers prefer white because it is easier to evaluate color schemes on a white background than on the traditional écru.

Penelope canvas is the traditional needlepoint canvas. It could have been called "duo" canvas, as the mesh, or spacing, of the weave is formed by the crossing of pairs of threads, or double threads. Stitches are taken on it diagonally across each intersection of these *double* threads. Double canvas is usually made of natural or écru-colored linen and is not as heavily starched as mono canvas. Recently, white double canvas has become available, though it is not always easy to find.

The "mesh size" of needlepoint canvas indicates how many stitches to the inch can be made on it. Since one stitch is made over each intersection of threads, the spacing, or mesh, of the threads determines the number of stitches per inch. Canvas comes in innumerable mesh sizes, some of the more common ones being 10, 12, and 14, meaning 10, 12, or 14 stitches to the inch. There is also a very coarse canvas called rug canvas which holds only 5 stitches to the inch and is ideal for children to work with. (I do not recommend that adults start on rug canvas, however. The change of pace when you begin a new project on finer canvas can be discouraging and a jolt.)

Penelope and mono canvas are worked exactly the same way: one stitch covers each intersection of threads. The difference is not in the working, but in the canvas. You must watch on the penelope that each stitch covers the cross made by the paired threads and does not "split" them. This is a little harder on the eyes than taking the stitch over the crossing of single threads on mono canvas, but if you have a piece of penelope before you, you can easily see that the pairs are placed close together in the weave and that they can be treated as one. Also, the vertical pairs are closer together than the horizontal pairs. It is very important that you always work penelope canvas with the closer pairs (those parallel to the selvage of the canvas) running up and down, not sideways, otherwise the stitches will slant incorrectly on the canvas and any geometrical pattern you try to count out on the canvas stitch for stitch will come out oblong instead of square. But a very real advantage of penelope is that the double weave fills the stitches so that the wool may "cover" better than on mono canvas —in other words, canvas threads are less likely to show through the wool stitching. If you are used to penelope, it is no harder to work on than mono; and the experts all say it is best for beginners to start on penelope. If you start on mono, getting used to the double mesh later is a nuisance.

Since mono canvas is a bit easier to see and therefore somewhat faster to work with, there is no reason not to use it if it suits your design and your wool covers it well. But it does have another disadvantage. This is that only one size of stitch can be made on mono. If it is coarse canvas, only large stitches can be made; if it is fine canvas, only small stitches can be made—a long, tedious job unless your project is a small one.

On penelope canvas, you can execute both large and small stitches. Once you have mastered the idea that penelope canvas is stitched on over pairs of threads, you can then reverse this idea and begin to separate the pairs and stitch over them singly—ignoring the pairing, separating the threads with your needle, and working the canvas as if it were a fine mono canvas. This means that in the same design you can have two very different sizes of stitches which create two very different moods. For example, on 10-mesh canvas, you can have a coarser background with 10 stitches to the inch and a delicate central design with 20 stitches to the inch. This is petit point.

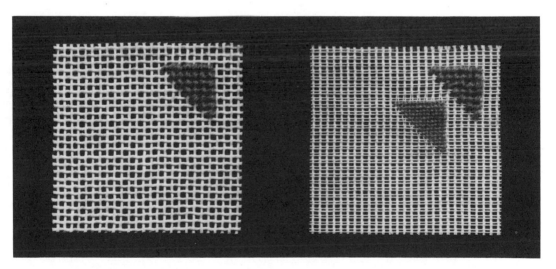

LEFT: *Mono canvas with basketweave stitch;* RIGHT: *Penelope canvas with basketweave stitch done in both needlepoint and petit point*

Petit point is usually stitched on penelope canvas. However, fine mono canvases are better if the whole piece is to be done in the small stitch. There are mono canvases 16, 18, 24, or even 32 stitches to the inch. There is no "official" stitch count at which needlepoint becomes petit point, but for most people 16- or 18-mesh mono canvases seem fine enough to be called petit-point canvas. Petit point, on either type of canvas, is no different and no more difficult than needlepoint (which Europeans call "gros point"). It is only smaller and slower. And petit point can do magical things to a design. More detail can be put into it and you may realize a true masterpiece. Always work the petit point *before* you stitch the coarser background around it. And it is much better to take the time to do some petit point in a design than to try to render too much detail on a coarse canvas.

When planning your own designs, which you will feel inspired to do after a while, consider the canvas size carefully. If you plan a design with a considerable amount of detail, choose a smaller-meshed canvas, but if you want to do a bold, simple design, use coarse canvas. This not only helps you to finish faster, but you will find that the bulkiness of the stitches adds a beautiful dimension to the design.

Finally, before beginning a piece of needlepoint, you must test the canvas with the type of wool you are planning to use to make sure that it is thick enough to cover the canvas completely. The effect you should achieve is plump, softly packed stitches. If they look lumpy, this means that the wool strand is too thick. If they are skinny and twisted and canvas shows through, you must make your strands thicker.

WOOL

Needlepoint wool is not the same as knitting worsted, although they may look similar. Needlepoint wool has long fibers which allow it to endure the tugging and pulling it is subjected to every time a stitch is made, while knitting wool has short fibers that will fray. Canvas is abrasive, but *good* needlepoint wool should not only endure the stitching process but survive better than the canvas.

The most common needlepoint wool is Persian wool—DMC and Paternayan being my favorite brands. Persian wool is "three ply," that is, three fine strands are loosely twisted together. This ply works well on coarse canvas (10-mesh). Or, the wool can be split to two strands for use on 12- or 14-mesh canvas, and it can be split to one strand for stitching petit point. Persian yarn comes in a broad range of colors and shades—more in some brands than in others.

Crewel Wool

Crewel wool is used primarily for crewel embroidery. It is finer than needlepoint wool, but it can be used on petit-point canvas. It, too, comes in a great variety of colors. The Safari Belt that appears on the jacket of this book and on page 122 is made with three strands of crewel wool on 16-mesh canvas.

Tapestry Wool

Tapestry wool is sold in department stores for use in filling in backgrounds of prepared needlepoint canvases—the kinds that have all the "fun stuff" done for you. Tapestry wool is a four-ply fiber which can be used whole on 12- or 14-mesh canvas or can be split into two strands for petit point, though it is somewhat inconvenient to split, being tightly twisted. There are brands of tapestry wool that come in unusual colors not available in Persian yarn, but in my opinion tapestry wool is not as luxurious or enjoyable to use.

Rug Wool

Rug wool is a coarse, rough-textured, three-ply yarn. It is sold by the pound (a small rug takes about four or five pounds of rug wool). It is used on very coarse canvases—8 stitches to the inch or less. As mentioned before, 5-mesh canvas and rug wool, because of their large size, are ideal to use for introducing children to needlepoint.

Other Needlepoint Fibers

There are several other fibers besides the traditional wool yarns that can be used for needlepoint. Petit-point embroidery done with silk threads on silk gauze is a very old European technique used by royalty for centuries. Only the best French silk really works well and it is expensive and not easy to find. Metallic threads that will not tarnish are a modern innovation that can add an exciting dimension to a design. (See Captain's Hat, page 40, and Mouse with Needle, page 42.)

How Much Wool Is Required?

Hope Hanley, in her excellent introductory book *Needlepoint*, has a chapter in which she gives complete mathematical formulas for measuring the amount of wool needed to cover a canvas. Some needlepoint shops even supply charts so that figuring can be done without much mental strain. However, perhaps because I don't care much for mathematics, I prefer simply to buy needlepoint wool by "feel."

When you go into a needlework shop, you will notice that experienced embroiderers and salespeople can look at a design and make an instinctive or "emotional" calculation as to how much wool will be needed. But people work differently: those who make a tight stitch will use less wool, sometimes as much as a third less, than those who make a loose stitch. As you do more and more needlepoint, you will learn to make these emotional calculations for yourself quite accurately. For your first project, take your design with you to the shop where you buy the wool. The salespeople will be most helpful in making any needed calculations.

My chief suggestion is that you always buy *more* wool than you think you need. You will always use up extra wool, especially when you start to experiment with color variations and ultimately with design variations of your own. Also, though wool manufacturers nowadays pride themselves on the fact that if you have the color numbers of the wools you buy, they can match them perfectly even in another dye lot, this is often more of an ideal than a fact. Though most needlepoint wool is sold by the ounce, some shops may be so willing to please that they will sell you as little as a strand if you run short, but don't count on it. Remember, it is especially in background stitching that the difference shows markedly if wool is used from two different dye lots that do not match perfectly.

NEEDLES

Needlepoint needles, called tapestry needles, are blunt and large-eyed and come in a variety of sizes to accommodate the full range of needlepoint canvases and wools. The largest is size 13, to be used with rug wool on rug canvas, and the smallest is size 24, to be used for petit point.

Canvas Size	Needle Size
5-mesh	#13
7-, 8-mesh	#15
10-, 12-, 14-mesh	#17 or #18
16-, 18-mesh	#19 or #20
Petit-point canvases	#21 to #24

You need to adjust the size of the needle to the size of the canvas you are using and to the wool that covers the canvas best. If you use too large a needle, you will have trouble pulling it through the mesh, which will not only slow up your work but will put extra strain on the wool and the canvas. If it is too small, you will have trouble threading it. Needles are inexpensive, so buy packages of a variety of sizes. Some manufacturers put needles of several sizes in one package. The best brands are English.

PLATE 1.
Opposite: Watermelon Wedge, page 30

PLATE 2.
Overleaf: Paisley Pillow—Light Against Dark, page 37

Good scissors are imperative. Get a pair of small, good-quality scissors—true embroidery scissors or even cuticle scissors—that are sharp and pointed so that you can trim off the tails of wool neatly on the back of the canvas when you finish off each strand. Canvas, however, should be cut with large sewing shears.

DESIGNS

First, of course, you must find a design you like, and the purpose of this book is to give you a big selection of professional designs to choose from. And some do-it-yourself steps have already been taken for you. The designs have been rendered in working line drawings. (This makes them much easier to transfer to canvas than many other design sources.) Then the color pictures of the finished designs show you exactly how they will look and—along with the numbered color keys given with each pattern—serve as a guide to color choices and placements throughout the whole project.

In using this book, you will do more of the planning yourself than if you bought the canvases already prepared for you. But you will be saving yourself a very considerable sum of money; and you will learn the few simple processes you need to know so that soon you will be able to adapt designs from other sources and even be inspired to create your own. Also, as you become a more accomplished embroiderer, you may want to use more drawings from this book, but to work the designs quite differently from the way they are shown in the color pictures.

TRANSFERRING THE DESIGN TO CANVAS

There are two ways to transfer patterns from this book to canvas: by *photostating* the drawing and then tracing it onto the canvas and by making a *free-hand graph* and tracing that onto the canvas. These procedures have to take place because, of necessity, most of the patterns have been reduced in size to fit them onto the printed page. (When you adapt your own designs from other sources, you will almost always find that the size has to be changed to suit your purpose, too.)

Photostating

Once you have chosen the design, check the dimensions of the original piece that are given with each pattern. To get back to the original dimensions—or to alter the pattern to any size you wish—have the pattern photostated right from the book. Photostating is an inexpensive commercial process by which line drawings can be enlarged, or reduced, to virtually any size you want. Look in the Yellow Pages under "Photo Copying" for the place nearest you. (Photocopying happens to be an entirely different process, and a photocopy is *not* what you want, but the same firms do both things and are usually listed under the general heading of "Photo Copying" in the phone book.)

Tell the shop exactly the dimensions you want the photostat of the drawing to be, and ask for a positive print. As I said, you can alter the dimensions given if you want. For example, the Paisley Pillow designed by Lou Gartner (page 37) could easily be blown up to make a small rug. Instructions for how to transfer your photostat to canvas begin on page 21.

Free-hand Graphing

If it is not convenient for you to get a photostat, you can use the old-fashioned method of free-hand graphing that needleworkers have been using for generations. Also, for simple designs, graphing can be so easy that getting a photostat is hardly worthwhile.

Cut a piece of good-quality tracing paper 7" x 10" (the size of the pages in this book), making sure the sides are parallel and all four corners are perfectly square. Make a ½" grid on the tracing paper: Mark dots ½" apart along all four sides, starting exactly ½" from the corners of the paper. Then, using a fine-line black marking pen and a ruler, connect the dots with black lines, first across the tracing paper and then up and down —and you have made a ½" grid!

Lay the grid over the pattern of your choice. You want it to stay put and not move; use a few dots of rubber cement, masking tape, or paper clips to make it hold still. The pattern now shows through the grid. If it doesn't show too clearly, trace the pattern lightly with pencil. (If the pattern you have chosen is printed across two facing pages of the book, you will see better how to join up the two halves if you make a ½" grid for both pages.)

Now your do-it-yourself ingenuity begins. Get a sheet of graph paper that is measured out in inches. Stationery stores carry inexpensive pads of this paper printed with either 8 or 10 little squares to the inch. Art-supply stores carry larger sheets. If your canvas will be larger than one sheet, tape sheets together, making sure that the grid meets on the inch lines. To explain what you do next, let's assume that you want to double the size of the drawing in the book. Every ½" on your homemade grid will equal 1" on your free-hand graph.

Starting at the upper right-hand corner of the graph paper, draw in the lines of the design free-hand. It sounds difficult in words, but it is simple to do: look at the position of a line in a ½" box on the grid, copy its position in the corresponding 1" box on the graph paper, and go on to the next box. Use a pencil and have an eraser handy, because you will undoubtedly start out by trial and error. When you have duplicated all the lines of the pattern, draw over them with a black marking pen and make the lines very bold.

If the enlargement you want to make is not as simple as merely doubling the size of the drawing, some arithmetic and a new, larger graph are required. Measure the width of the drawing in the book. Perhaps that is 6". You want the needlepoint to be 18" wide. Divide 6 into 18, which equals 3. This means that the squares on your big free-hand graph should be three times as big as the ½" squares on your little grid. Three times ½" equals 1½". So, on the graph paper, make your own new large grid with a marking pen, spacing the lines 1½" apart. It is convenient to measure this out on graph paper because the paper is already ruled to help keep things straight, but it can just as well be done on a plain sheet of drawing paper.

Even if you don't quite get the arithmetic above, just follow instructions exactly, no matter what different dimensions you are working with: Measure the width of the drawing. Divide that into the width you want for the finished needlepoint. Multiply ½" by *that* figure. The result is the dimension of the squares on the new large grid that you will draw.

Then, redraw the pattern itself onto the large grid as explained before.

Free-hand graphing is not recommended for very intricate patterns. There is too much detail in each square which is hard to redraw on the large graph. One way to get around this is to start with a small ¼" grid— instead of ½"—laid over the drawing in the book. But this can become laborious and confusing and finding a photostat shop to do the enlarging is the best solution.

Stitch-for-Stitch Graphing

A few of the designs in this book are drawn stitch for stitch on graphs and do not need to be traced onto the canvas; indeed, they shouldn't be. These patterns are worked by counting out the stitches for each color on the canvas as they appear on the graphed drawing. You work directly from the book. As you will see, these designs are geometrical repeat patterns, so the stitch counting is easy. Each square on the graph equals one stitch. When you have stitched the repeat motif once or twice, you do not even have to refer to the drawing again. Just copy the motif already on your canvas (but be sure every stitch is in the right place first!)

Tracing the Pattern Onto the Canvas

Once you have arrived at a life-size pattern, either by photostating or free-hand graphing, you are ready to put it on the canvas.

First you must prepare your canvas. Home sewers will appreciate the importance of the placement of the warp and woof threads. As with any fabric, the warp threads (those parallel to the selvage) must run up and down the canvas, not across it. This is imperative for double canvas, but the warp threads are very easy to see because they are the pairs of threads set closer together in the weave. On mono canvas, the direction of the weave is less important and, also, which is woof and which is warp is impossible to see after the selvage is cut off. Print the word "top" on your piece of mono canvas before you cut so you won't forget which end is up!

Cut your canvas so there will be a good 2" or more of extra canvas all around the finished piece. Take wide masking tape and fold it over the edges to keep them from fraying.

Now, tape the photostat or free-hand graph to a flat surface. Center the canvas over the drawing, and tape down the top edge only. Don't tape it all the way around, as you'll probably want to lift it up a number of times to check that you're getting all the lines onto the canvas as you trace. The drawing underneath should show well through the canvas, because the photostat will be bold or you will have made your graph drawing bold.

Trace the design onto the canvas with an *indelible* marking pen (I recommend AD markers), using a neutral, not too dark color, such as gray. I emphasize *indelible* for a very good reason. If the ink is not waterproof, it will bleed through your stitching when you block the canvas, and your fine work will be irreparably ruined. Test the marker before you begin by making lines on a small piece of canvas and then scrubbing the canvas with soap and warm water. No lesser test is acceptable. If the ink runs in the slightest, look for another marker. For final security, I also recommend spraying the canvas with a fixative (Krylon by Borden, Inc., or Myplar by M. Grumbacher, Inc.). These can be bought at any art-supply store and come in spray cans. These are very important precautions; a ruined piece of needlepoint is heartbreaking after all that work!

Finally, you may want to use a few of the patterns the same size as they are printed in the book (such as the belts or Christmas ornaments). It is inconvenient to put the canvas directly on the book for tracing, and you could spoil your canvas. Trace the whole design onto tracing paper first, then trace onto your canvas from that.

Working Out the Color Scheme

If you want to copy the designs in this book as they were made originally, the color scheme is all done for you. Each pattern has its list of numbered colors, and the numbers on the drawings tell you where to put each color. The color pictures tell you the effect you will achieve.

However, when you buy your wool colors, remember that it isn't really possible to match the wools precisely with what you see in the printed color picture. Choose approximately the same colors, of about the same lightness, darkness, and brightness, and then look at the wools all together to see if they look good together. It will take a few adjustments before they do. Be sure for large areas such as backgrounds that you choose a version of the color in the picture that you really like. Also be sure that the colors that you can tell from the picture should contrast with each other or blend together give the same effect in the actual wools. These effects are much more important than matching the colors in the picture. Check with the color list given with the pattern to see that you have everything you need.

If you want to make up a new color scheme of your own, test it *before* you trace the design onto the canvas. The first thing to do is to trace your enlarged drawing onto good tracing paper, in pencil. Put this tracing on a white surface and experiment with colored pencils, poster paints, or acrylic paints. (You must not experiment on the original drawing, as you need this for getting the pattern onto canvas, and you may also need it to trace off again for another experimental color scheme.) Don't be concerned with every detail; you will work these out with the wool colors later on.

When you have the colors planned in a general way, you can do several things. Once you have traced the original pattern onto the canvas with a gray marking pen, you can simply refer to your colored tracing for the position of the colors. Or, when you trace the design onto the canvas, instead of using gray, outline each area with its own color (again with *indelible* fine-line marking pens). Often this is all the color indication a canvas needs. With your colored paper pattern to refer to and your color-keyed canvas as guides, you can then easily "paint in" with wool.

If you prefer to work on a canvas that has all the color painted in first, use acrylic paints that are labeled "insoluble after drying" (not all are so labeled). Any art-supply store carries them. They are easy to use and come in a wide range of colors in jars or tubes. Remember that no paint will exactly match the color of the wool—and no paint needs to. You need only a general effect. (It *is* important not to make the paint any darker than the wool to be used over it or it will show through.) Paint on the canvas is a help in preventing the canvas itself from showing between stitches that may not cover it too well, and this is one of the advantages of painted canvases. Remember, however, that though people do seem to feel "safer" working on a painted canvas, in actual fact the paint may make the work harder to see and the true effect of the wool colors harder to evaluate as you work.

In any event, before painting a canvas, trace the drawing onto it with a gray marker first, then fill in with your acrylic colors. If you want only to sketch in the colors lightly, you can use blunt-ended indelible markers instead. Fixative is recommended for all painted-in canvases.

STITCHES

For the purposes of this book, I will describe only two stitches, the continental or tent stitch and the basketweave stitch. All of the designs in the book can be executed with only these stitches. (On some patterns, bargello and other stitches are suggested by the designers. Many needle-pointers already know these very lovely stitches, and descriptions of them can be found in any number of other needlepoint books. In the Bibliography, I have listed some of my favorites.)

First, there are three simple things beginners need to learn.

To thread the needle: Do not attempt to push the end of a piece of wool into the eye of the needle as you normally do with sewing thread. It will not work. Fold the end of the piece of wool, and push the folded end into the eye.

To start a piece of wool: Make a knot at the end of the piece of wool. Insert the needle into the canvas from the *front*, an inch or more from the point where you will make your first stitch. The stitching will cover the loose tail of wool on the back and lock it into place. When the stitching reaches the knot on the front of the canvas, snip it off. There must never be any knots in needlepoint, not even on the back of the canvas.

To finish a piece of wool: Run your needle under stitches on the back of the canvas for an inch or more, and trim the wool off closely.

THE CONTINENTAL STITCH

The continental stitch is the simplest of the two basic needlepoint stitches. It is used for outlining shapes and filling in very small areas. (In directions for working patterns I usually suggest that you outline first with the continental stitch.) I firmly believe that you should *never* fill in a background or any large area with continental. Because both the back and front of the stitch are diagonal, large areas of it will pull the canvas out of shape, and a lot of blocking will be required to pull it square again. And sometimes such a piece of needlepoint will either not remain in shape (you've seen those lopsided pillows) or cannot be pulled into shape at all.

You start any needlepoint stitch by first pulling the wool up from the back of the canvas. Make the continental stitch by crossing over the intersection of a vertical and a horizontal thread of the canvas—the direction of the stitch is always from lower left to upper right—and bring your needle up ready for the next stitch in the space to the left of the space from which you started the first stitch. The stitches accumulate horizontally from right to left. When you come to the end of your row, if you want to put another row underneath it, you must turn the canvas upside-down.

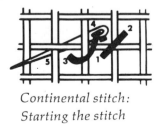

Continental stitch: Starting the stitch

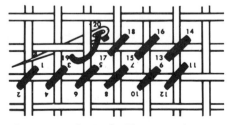

Continental stitch: Turning the corner—stitches 11/12 and 13/14

Outlining with the Continental

Outlining is not done for tiny patches of color (which are simply filled in with continental); but to make the shapes of definite areas of color follow smoothly the lines of the pattern on the canvas, it is often advisable to outline the areas with their colors before filling them in. (A specific exception: geometric patterns—these are worked all in basketweave.) You *always* begin at the *upper right* of the area. First, follow the outline leftward horizontally with the continental. Then, when the outline bends either upward or downward and still to the left, make short little rows of the continental that follow along the pattern line drawn on the canvas. Sometimes the outline, as it moves up and left, requires a few basketweave stitches which accumulate diagonally up the canvas (see page 25); or, if it moves diagonally left and down, it may require a row of single stitches that are just like the ordinary back stitch in sewing. Or, the outline will require that you place some stitches vertically downward, one under the next.

Eventually, the outline will bend back to the right; at this point it may again need a few basketweave stitches, which this time accumulate diagonally downward and to the right (see page 25). Or, finally, the outline may require that you work again horizontally, but this time from left to right. Since the continental will not go in this direction, you must turn the canvas completely upside-down, and then you will be able to follow the outline again back to the point where you began it.

If at any time you become confused about which direction the canvas should be turned for outlining, do this: Look at the place where you began, where the stitches are correctly slanted from lower left to upper right. Now look at the place where you are stitching: If you cannot take your next stitch 1) where you want to take it, 2) take it from lower left to upper right over the intersection of canvas threads, and 3) also produce a stitch that slants in exactly the same direction on the canvas as your original correct stitches—then you need to turn the canvas upside-down and the next stitch will be correct. (In fact, this same test applies when you are filling in with continental as well as outlining.)

No matter what stitch you may be doing on the canvas—continental, outlining, basketweave—all must slant in the same direction. When the canvas is finished, all the stitches will look alike and you will not be able to tell from the front how they were made.

When the outline of an area is finished, fill it in with basketweave.

Some expert needlepointers can fill in quite complicated patterns without outlining the color areas first and fill them in directly with the basketweave. This is good if you are sure of what you are doing. But if the outline becomes ragged and strays too far from the pattern on the canvas, you have a lot of stitches to take out to repair it, while the outline of a single row of continental can be done easily by trial and error because there are few stitches to take out and do over.

THE BASKETWEAVE STITCH

The basketweave stitch seems at first harder to do than the continental, but it is much the most useful stitch and no harder when you are used to it. It is used for filling in backgrounds as well as any other areas of any size. Because only the front of the stitch is diagonal and the back of it is straight, it does not pull the canvas out of shape as much as the continental; expert stitchers can keep a canvas almost perfectly square using a maximum of basketweave. The straightness of the stitch on the back of the canvas gives a perfectly woven look that gives it its name. Like the continental, it is a well-padded stitch on the back of the canvas which makes the needlepoint very durable. Another advantage of basketweave is that you can work it without turning the canvas upside-down to start a new row of stitches.

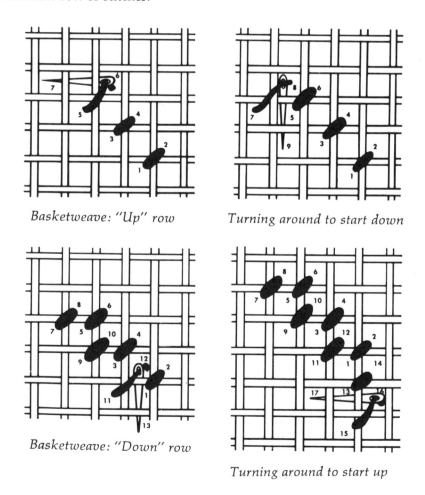

Basketweave: "Up" row Turning around to start down

Basketweave: "Down" row

Turning around to start up

The best way to learn the basketweave is from a diagram, as words make the whole thing sound much more complicated than it is. The stitches are worked in diagonal rows. In the diagrams below, the odd numbers represent the spaces in which the needle comes up from the back to the front of the canvas. The even numbers represent the spaces in which the needle goes in from the front to the back of the canvas.

A hint about working this stitch on mono canvas: When you are working the "up" row, make sure your stitch is made over an intersection of canvas thread in which the woof, or horizontal thread, is on top. When working a "down" row, make your stitch over an intersection of canvas threads in which the warp, or vertical thread, is on top. If you stitch one row correctly, the one next to it coming back the other way will automatically be correct. Do this consistently (check each time you start a new row or a new strand of wool), and the wool will cover the canvas much better; and strange, diagonal ridges will be kept at a minimum in large areas of stitching.

Often in working a design, you will find that you come across small areas where you cannot put in the stitches in the sequence of a true basketweave or continental. While it is important, somewhat, to keep the back of your canvas as neat as possible to prevent lumps and bumps from forming, if you must skip about a little across the back of the canvas to put colors in their right places, don't worry about it. Just don't pull too hard and make sure the stitches on the front always slant in the same direction.

FINISHING YOUR NEEDLEPOINT

BLOCKING

Once you have finished your canvas, you must block it so that it returns to its original shape.

Before you block the needlepoint, check to see if it needs cleaning. If it does, you may do a couple of things. First, to remove just superficial spots or soil, use a cleaning spray such as K2r by Texize; directions are on the label. Or, you may do a more thorough job by soaking the piece in cold water and Woolite or Ivory soap. If you think the piece actually needs scrubbing, scrub only from the back, squeezing the suds through. Do not scrub the front of the piece or the stitches will fuzz up and lose their smooth texture.

After washing, let the piece dry before you stretch it; needlepoint is easier to handle dry than wet. If you have not washed it, stretch it dry and wet it later. Lay the needlepoint on a clean board made of soft wood or composition board that tacks will go into easily. Always block needlepoint face *down*, which will even up the surface of the stitching.

If there is plenty of extra canvas around the stitching, you can tack it to the board with anything you want, even carpet tacks, as any rust marks will disappear when the piece is mounted or upholstered. If the tacks must be put in quite close to the stitching, don't take chances. Use rustproof thumbtacks or pushpins. (Pushpins cost the most, but they are very easy to use.)

Tack the four corners of the canvas so that the sides are parallel and the corners are at right angles. Pull the canvas as you do this to get it taut. (It will not lie flat yet.) Now stretch the canvas and tack it at the center of each side. Continue stretching and tacking all the way around until the tacks are about ½" apart, or closer, and the whole canvas lies absolutely flat. Then, thoroughly soak the needlepoint with a clean sponge and cold water. If the canvas is very badly out of shape, you can dampen it on the board before you finish tacking it; this will make it limp so that it can be made to lie flat as you stretch it.

MOUNTING AND UPHOLSTERING

If you are a home sewer, mounting and upholstering your own work can be a rewarding challenge. However, after so much work has been put into a piece of needlepoint, most people want their pieces mounted or upholstered professionally. In the section of this book entitled Shops and Designers on page 173, I have noted those that will mount and upholster needlepoint for you. Some will accept needlepoint by mail if explicit directions accompany the piece. However, check also the needlework shops in your area. For upholstering furniture, your local upholsterer can certainly do the work. Most upholsterers will block the needlepoint that they mount for you.

Patterns

WATERMELON WEDGE

NEEDLE IN A HAYSTACK
Dallas, Texas

DESIGNER: *Joyce Terrell*

Color page 17.

6½" x 7" overall; #10 mono canvas; 3-strand Paternayan Persian yarn

This unique little pillow is one of the finest in our collection. Its beauty is in the construction of the wedge. The watermelon pattern is stitched within a lopsided oval, as shown in the drawing, which curves over the top of the wedge. The rind is green corduroy with self-welting—a rewarding challenge to the home seamstress.

WATERMELON WEDGE — *color key*

1 *Deep Cadmium Red*
2 *Black*
3 *Pale Lime-Green*
4 *Kelly Green or Chartreuse*

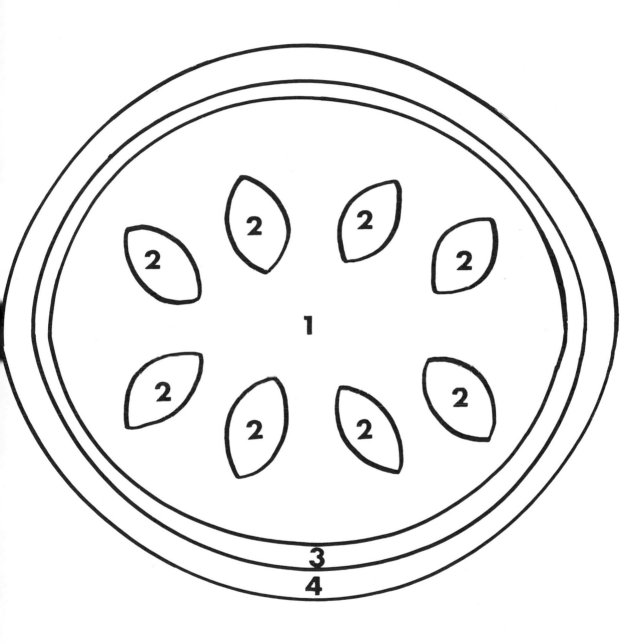

31

LOBSTER

DEE NEEDLEPOINT ORIGINALS
Point Pleasant Beach, New Jersey

DESIGNER: *Dee Norton*

Color page 35.

14" x 14" not including border; #12 mono canvas; 3-strand Persian yarn split to 2 strands

This design is ideal for a den or boat. Outline the lobster in continental stitch and fill in with basketweave. When the lobster motif is finished, begin working the gingham-design background.

Three colors are used for the background: red, white, and a shade of pink achieved by combining two strands of white with one strand of red. Working horizontally, create a row of red and pink "boxes" or squares, any size you wish. Then work a second row of squares, this time alternating pink and white squares. Repeat these rows until the background is filled.

LOBSTER — *color key*

1 *Black*
2 *Cadmium Red*
3 *White*

PAISLEY PILLOW—LIGHT AGAINST DARK

NEEDLEPOINT DESIGN
Palm Beach, Florida, &
New York, New York

DESIGNER: *Lou Gartner*

Color page 18.

14½″ x 14½″ not including border; #14 mono canvas; 3-strand Persian yarn split to 2 strands

Paisley designs are ideal for using up wool colors left over from previous projects. A color plan is needed: a) light and bright design against dark, as here (or the reverse, dark and bright against light); b) "feathers" all worked in the same color scheme (such as colors 2 through 5); c) remaining motifs worked in an assortment of colors, with most of these repeated several times and repeating feather colors as well. The fun is in your combining the colors you have. However, those used in the pillow in the color picture are listed below if you wish to copy it.

Because of the many curved lines, see advice on page 24 for outlining shapes before filling in colors. A half-inch or more of border should be stitched around the whole design as seam allowance for upholstering.

PAISLEY PILLOW — *color key*

BACKGROUND:
1 *Black*

"FEATHERS":
2 *Lemon Yellow*
3 *Mustard Gold*
4 *White*
5 *Corn Yellow*

OTHER COLORS:
Ice Blue
Pea Green
Jade Green
Moss Green
Strong Blue-Green
Bright Purple
Orange
Brick Orange
Brick Red
Pearl Pink
Cream

CAPTAIN'S HAT

DEE NEEDLEPOINT ORIGINALS
Point Pleasant Beach, New Jersey

DESIGNER: *Dee Norton*

Color page 35.

14" x 14" not including border; #12 mono canvas; 3-strand Persian yarn split to 2 strands

Here again is an effective combination of Persian and metallic threads. When using metallic thread, you should place a small amount of glue at the end of the thread to keep it from unraveling. Outline all areas in black using the continental stitch, then fill in with basketweave.

This is just one of a series of hat pillows available from the designer. There is also a fireman's hat and a Scottish tam. Part of the charm of the design is the outline of a nose coming down from the brim of the hat. You might want to stitch a name and date into the design.

CAPTAIN'S HAT — *color key*

1 *Black*
2 *White*
3 *Cadmium Yellow*
4 *Metallic Gold*
5 *Royal Blue*

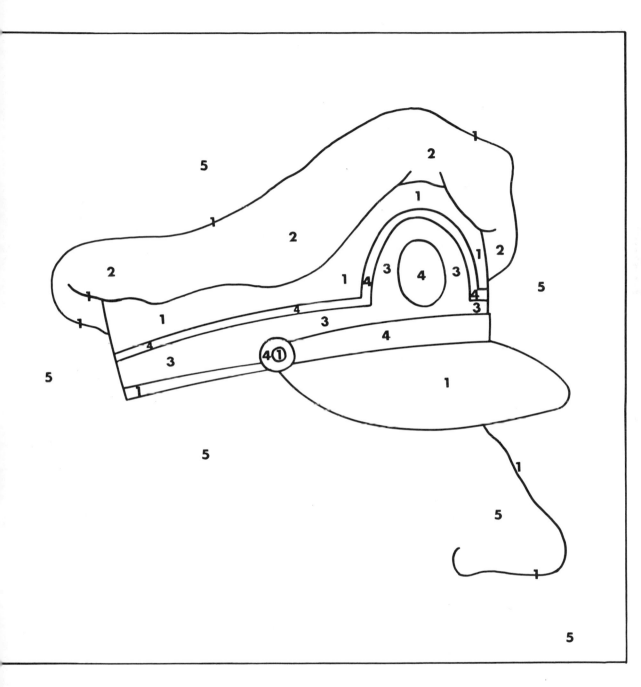

41

MOUSE WITH NEEDLE

DEE NEEDLEPOINT ORIGINALS
Point Pleasant Beach, New Jersey

DESIGNER: *Dee Norton*

Color page 36.

14½" x 12½" not including border; #12 mono canvas; 3-strand Persian yarn split to 2 strands

There are interesting subtleties throughout this design. The coloration in the ears, around the nose, and on the belly is very soft. Outline the entire mouse in cool gray using the continental stitch, then fill in the shading with basketweave. The background can be done in any number of bargello stitches or in simple basketweave. Note that the needle is done entirely in gold metallic thread, creating an interesting change in texture.

MOUSE WITH NEEDLE — *color key*

1 *Deep Coral*
2 *Dark Cool Gray*
3 *Gold Metallic*
4 *White*
5 *Pale Pink*
6 *Ultra Pale Brown*
7 *Pale Warm Gray*
8 *Black*

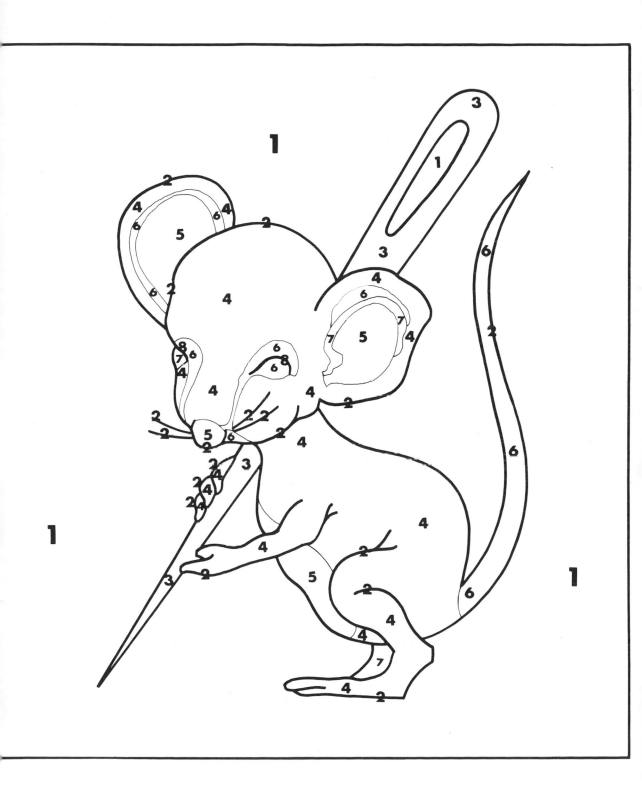

PLATE 5.
Opposite: Owl, page 52

PLATE 6.
Overleaf: Knockout Scene, page 54; Fairy Tale Scene, page 49

PLATE 7.
Color Page 47: Amanda, page 59

PLATE 8.
Color Page 48: Treetops, page 62; Block Design (Clemson), page 64

44

FAIRY TALE SCENE

SOOKIE SOLON DESIGNS
New York, New York

DESIGNER: *Sookie Solon*

Color page 46.

14½" x 14½" not including border; #10 mono canvas; 3-strand French or Persian yarn split to 2 strands

This canvas gives the feeling of a stained-glass window. To achieve this effect, outline all the colored areas in black using the continental stitch. Fill in the bold colors with basketweave. The simple stitch gives the design the flat appearance and enhances its stained-glass quality.

FAIRY TALE SCENE — *color key*

   1   *Light Rose*
   2   *Light Pink*
   3   *Gold*
   4   *Powder Blue*
   5   *Deep Powder Blue*
   6   *Dark Brown*
   7   *Light Olive*
   8   *Forest Green*
   9   *Chartreuse*
  10   *White*
  11   *Black*

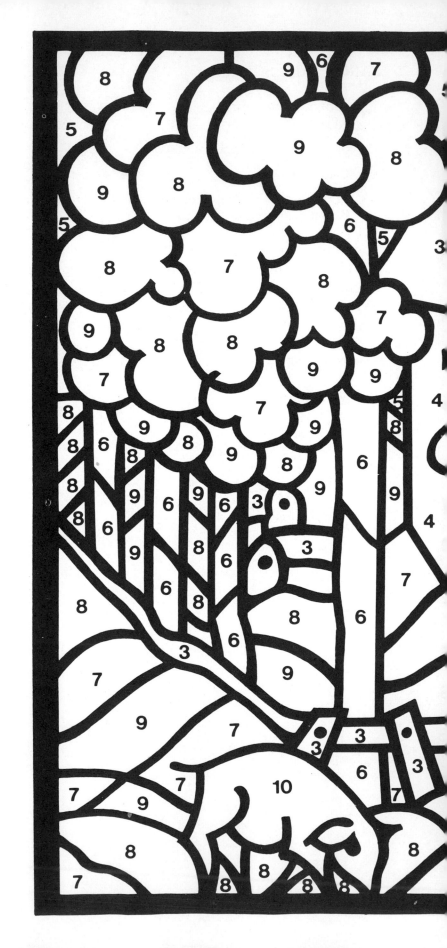

51

OWL

DA NEEDLEPOINT
Far Rockaway, New York

DESIGNER: *Dennis M. Arnold*

Color page 45.

17½" x 19½"; #12 mono canvas; 3-strand French or Persian yarn split to 2 strands

This design is ideal for experimenting with many different types of needlepoint stitches of your own choosing. These stitches are easily mastered by reading any one of several good needlepoint instruction books (see Bibliography). Color is very important to this design; follow the color directions carefully, otherwise the design will become too abstract.

owl — *color key*

1	*Cadmium Orange*
2	*Cadmium Yellow*
3	*Light Orange*
4	*Pale White*
5	*Light Purple*
6	*Deep Purple*
7	*Light Yellow*
8	*Deep Magenta*
9	*Pale Yellow*
10	*Dark Brown*
11	*Brown*
12	*Steel Blue or Gray Blue*
13	*Pale Blue*
14	*True Blue*
15	*Light Blue*
16	*Chartreuse*
17	*Pink*
18	*Royal Green*

KNOCKOUT SCENE

SOOKIE SOLON DESIGNS
New York, New York

DESIGNER: *Sookie Solon*

Color page 46.

13" x 13" not including border; #10 mono canvas; 3-strand French or Persian yarn. Design may be ordered in kit form.

The unique features of this design are the blending of one color into another to create depth and the fact that you may combine one strand of wool with a metallic thread to create a glow in the canvas. Outline all of the colored areas in black using the continental stitch. Fill in the colored areas with basketweave.

KNOCKOUT SCENE — *color key*

 1 *Beige*
 2 *Cadmium Red combined with Metallic Red*
 3 *Cadmium Orange combined with Metallic Goldenrod*
 4 *Deep Magenta*
 5 *Cadmium Yellow*
 6 *Pink*
 7 *Flesh*
 8 *Chartreuse*
 9 *Olive*
10 *Citron*
11 *Royal Purple*
12 *Light Purple*
13 *Light Maroon*
14 *Process Blue*
15 *Light Blue*
16 *True Blue*
17 *Pale Blue*

AMANDA

SOOKIE SOLON DESIGNS
New York, New York

DESIGNER: *Sookie Solon*

Color page 47.

13" x 13" not including border; #12 mono canvas; 3-strand French or Persian yarn split to 2 strands

The trick to this design is the black outline around each color area. The outline should be done in the simple continental stitch and the colored areas should be filled in with basketweave. A one-inch border of black should be stitched around the whole design to allow for framing or upholstering.

AMANDA — *color key*

1 *Acid Green*
2 *Pink*
3 *Yellow*
4 *Powder Blue*
5 *Light Purple*
6 *Rose*
7 *Cadmium Red*
8 *Golden Tan*
9 *Periwinkle Blue*
10 *Flesh*
11 *Black*

TREETOPS

CREATIVE STITCHERY
Philadelphia, Pennsylvania

DESIGNER: *Creative Stitchery*

Color page 48.

14" x 14" overall dimensions; #12 mono canvas; 3-strand Persian yarn split to 2 strands

This Op Art design is outlined in a fine black line done in continental stitch. The colored areas are executed in basketweave. Use one basic family of colors throughout. The red family is used in the sample, color page 48, but you might try using vivid greens or bright blues. The colors outlined in black create a very strong design.

TREETOPS — *color key*

1. *Black*
2. *White*
3. *Purple*
4. *Golden Orange*
5. *Deep Magenta*
6. *Shocking Pink*
7. *Pink*

BLOCK DESIGN (Clemson)

ROBIN HOOD WOOL SHOP
Clemson, South Carolina

DESIGNER: *Marion E. Scoular*

Color page 48.

12″ x 12″ overall design; #10 double (penelope) canvas; 3-strand DMC or Persian yarn

This is an ideal design for graphing. (See Stitch-for-Stitch Graphing, page 21.) The three-dimensional quality of the design is achieved through the careful use of color. The entire design can be stitched in basketweave, or you may work a different bargello stitch on each plane of the cube. If you wish to stitch letters into the design, use basketweave on the plane where the initials appear. Make sure the letters are centered.

BLOCK DESIGN (CLEMSON) — *color key*

◻	1	*Pumpkin*
○	2	*Cadmium Orange*
/	3	*Light Purple or Pink*
/	4	*Dark Purple*

Letters in the name are done in *Dark Purple*.

GOLD MEDALLION (Scroll Wall Hanging)

NEEDLE IN A HAYSTACK
Dallas, Texas

DESIGNER: *Jahn*

Color page 58.

18″ x 18″ not including border; #10 mono canvas; 3-strand Persian yarn

This beautiful wall hanging may be made larger by continually repeating the pattern. It is done in the simple continental and basket-weave stitches throughout. Any choice of curtain rod may be used to support the piece, or the tabs may be eliminated and the design can then be upholstered or framed.

GOLD MEDALLION — *color key*

1 *Beige or Cream*
2 *Light Gold*
3 *Medium Gold*
4 *Deep Gold*
5 *Dark Brown*

OP BLOCKS INLAID IN 9 COLORS

DESIGNER: *Narcisse Chamberlain*

Color page 57.

13¾" x 13¾" not including background border; #10 mono canvas; 3-strand Persian yarn

This design should not be drawn on the canvas; it is simply copied stitch for stitch on blank canvas from the graph, entirely in basket-weave. Each square on the graph equals 1 stitch. Once you have copied the upper right-hand block from the graph, you can copy the next blocks from the one already stitched—rather than always referring to the graph. However, be sure to follow the graph for the outside edges of the overall block pattern and for the frame, because the way these join together is different on all four sides. The plain off-white background border (not drawn) must be at least 8 stitches wide, or more, as seam allowance for pillow upholstery.

The rows of blocks can easily be added to or shortened in either direction to change the shape of the needlepoint from square to oblong; the center sections on each side of the frame can be lengthened or shortened (or eliminated) accordingly. Variations on this block-and-frame design work especially well for upholstery for director's chairs; adjust the width of the background border to arrive at exactly the required dimensions.

OP BLOCKS INLAID IN 9 COLORS — *color key*

1	*Shell Pink*
2	*Rose Pink*
3	*Coral Rose*
4	*Red Rose*
5	*Fuchsia*
6	*Red Orange*
7	*Orange*
8	*Bright Yellow*
9	*Pale Yellow*
10	*Light Gray-Blue*
11	*Dark Gray-Blue*
12	*Black*
13	*Pure White*
14	*Off-White*

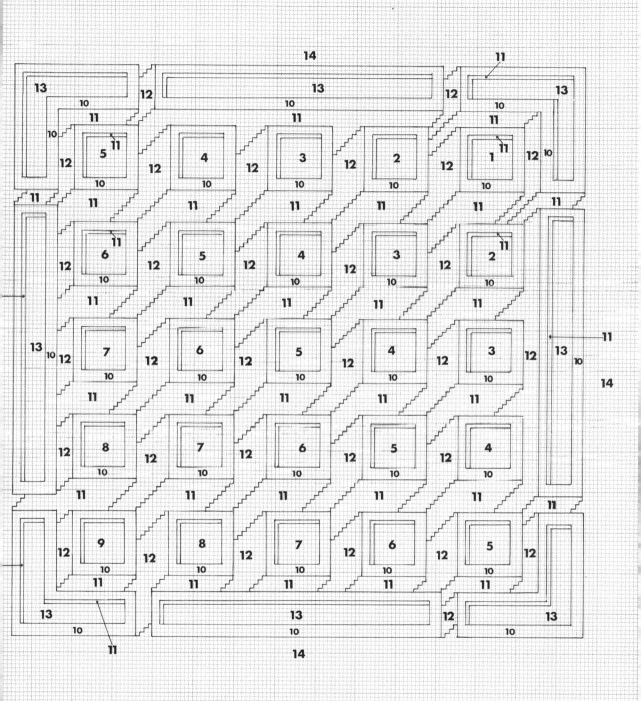

BUTTERFLY REPEAT

NEEDLE IN A HAYSTACK
Dallas, Texas

DESIGNER: *Joyce Terrell*

Color page 75.

13" x 13" overall; #14 mono canvas; 3-strand Persian yarn split to 2 strands

This pattern may be expanded for a larger pillow by adding rows of butterflies in any direction. If you do not want a monochromatic color scheme, brighter colors will work just as well. It is suggested that plain continental and basketweave stitches be used throughout.

BUTTERFLY REPEAT — *color key*

1 *Avocado Green, Light*
2 *Medium Aqua*
3 *Light Lime-Green*
4 *Pale Process Blue*
5 *Royal Blue*
6 *Winter Green*
7 *Off-White or Light Beige*

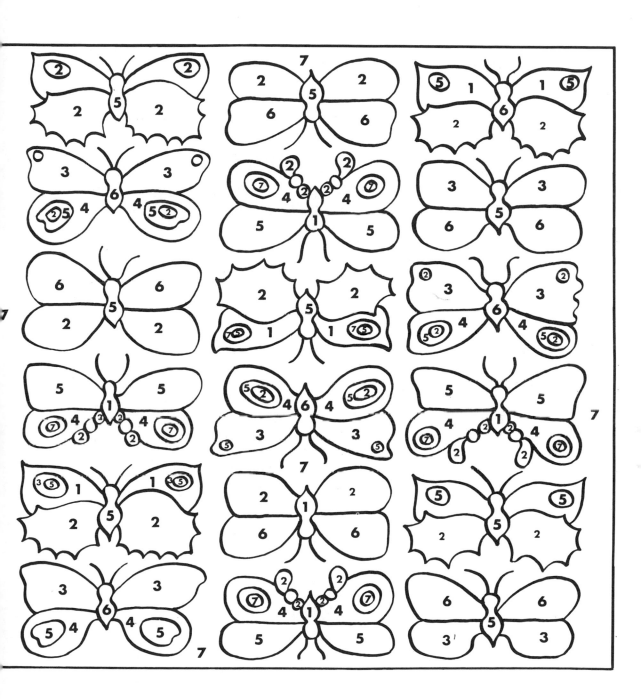

PINEAPPLE MOTIF

NEEDLEPOINT, INC.
New Orleans, Louisiana

DESIGNER: *Mrs. Robert Howard*

Color page 75.

14" x 14" not including border; #14 mono canvas; 3-strand Persian yarn split to 2 strands

This design has an unusual translucent effect, achieved through the careful use of a monochromatic color scheme that makes it appear as though one of the pineapples is placed on top of the other. Outline all color areas in continental stitch and fill in with basketweave.

PINEAPPLE MOTIF — *color key*

Pineapple
1   Deep Rust
2   Medium Rust
3   Medium Gold
4   Cadmium Yellow
5   Light Yellow

Leaves
6   Dark Emerald-Green
7   Deep Teal-Blue
8   Medium Green
9   Royal Blue

Crisscross marking
10   Dark Brown

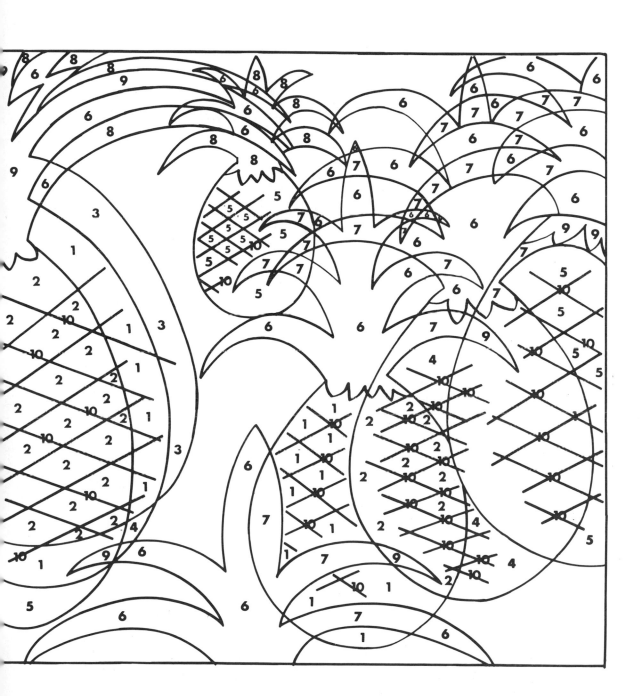

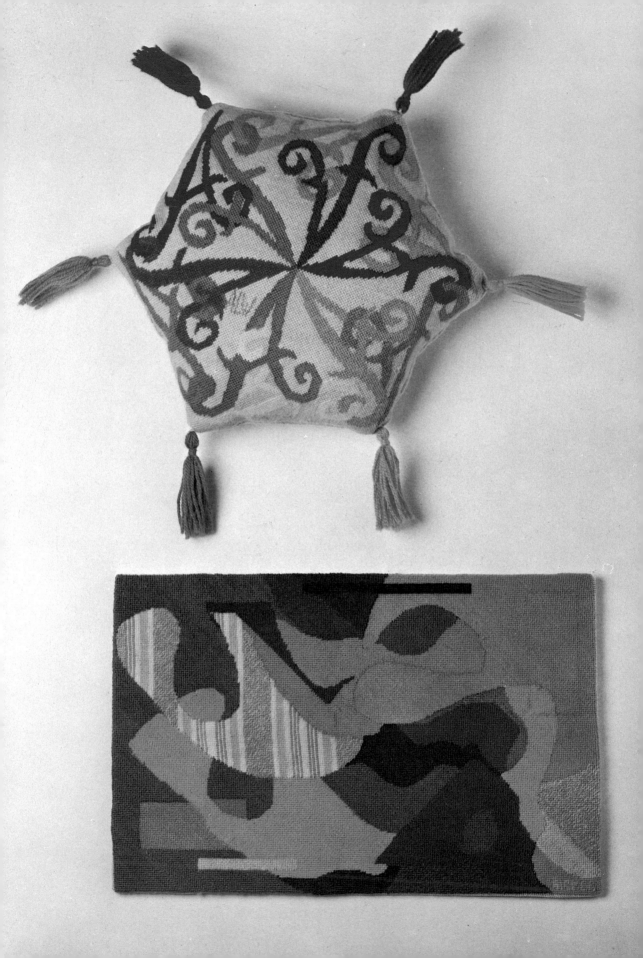

ORIENTAL RECTANGLE

THE OPEN DOOR TO STITCHERY
Great Neck, New York

DESIGNER: *The Open Door to Stitchery*

Color page 58.

12" x 16" overall dimensions; #12 mono canvas; 3-strand Persian yarn split to 2 strands

The success of this design is achieved through combining a simple color design with interesting bargello stitches. A list of the stitches used is found with the color list. Highlighting areas with silver metallic thread adds to the beauty of the design.

ORIENTAL RECTANGLE — *color key*

1 *Cool Dark Gray* (horizontal Scotch stitch)
2 *Cool Medium Gray* (horizontal Scotch stitch)
3 *Silver*
4 *Off White or Cream* (bargello stitch—pattern outline)
5 *Cadmium Red* (horizontal Scotch stitch)

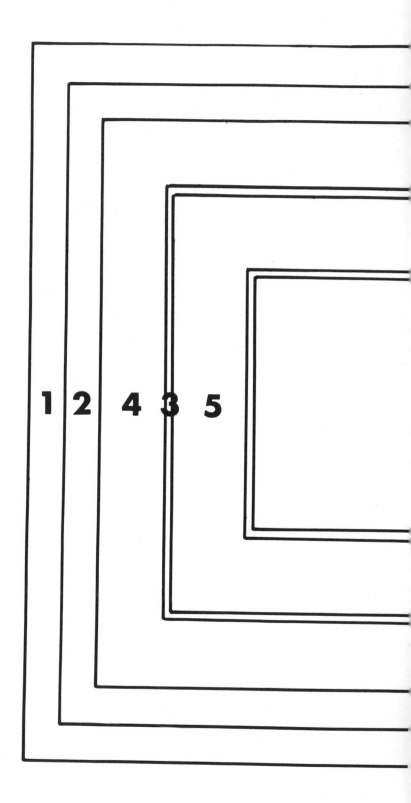

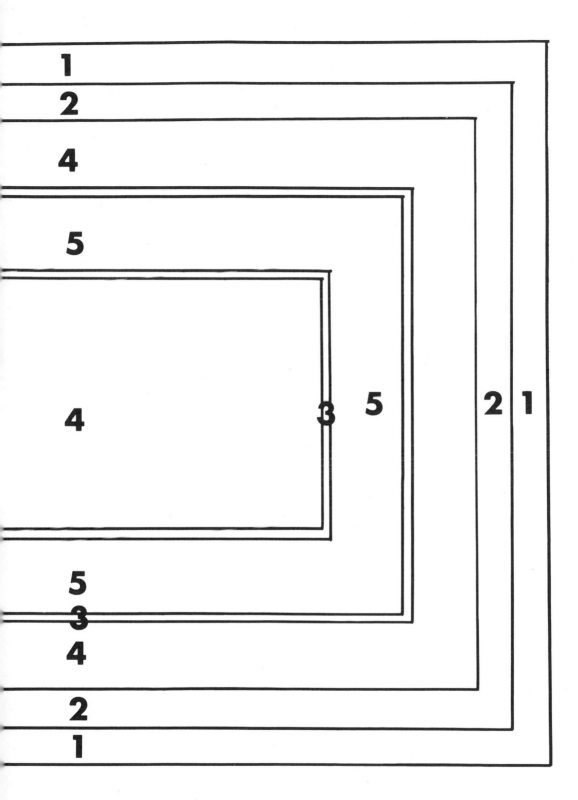

MOD MONOGRAMS

SIGN OF THE ARROW
St. Louis, Missouri

DESIGNER: *Linde Wiedow*

Color page 76.

13½" hexagon; #12 mono canvas; 3-strand Persian yarn split to 2 strands

This design is an interesting variation on the monogram motif, in this instance using the letter A. Outline the colored areas with continental stitch and fill in with basketweave. The upholstering of the pillow should be done carefully to preserve its hexagonal shape. The tassels are optional.

MOD MONOGRAMS—*color key*

1 *Royal Blue*
2 *Deep Rust*
3 *Apple Green*
4 *Turquoise*
5 *Burnt Orange*
6 *Kelly Green*
7 *Light Yellow-Green*
8 *Process Blue*
9 *Melon*
10 *Bright Baby Blue*
11 *Olive*
12 *Cadmium Red*
13 *Cadmium Yellow*

81

ABSTRACT

AMERICAN CREWEL & CANVAS STUDIOS
Denville, New Jersey

DESIGNER: *Nancy Rickert*

Color page 76.

18″ x 12″ overall dimensions; #12 mono canvas; 3-strand DMC or Persian yarn split to 2 strands

This abstract design may be stitched using the color scheme shown, or it can easily be worked using a variety of other colors. The salt-and-pepper feeling of the design is achieved by working certain areas with a multicolored thread made by combining one strand of a light color with one strand of a dark color. Outline each area with continental stitch and fill in with basketweave.

ABSTRACT — *color key*

1 *White*
2 *Cadmium Yellow*
3 *Deep Yellow*
4 Combine one strand *Cadmium Yellow* with one strand *Yellow Green*
5 *Navy Blue*
6 *Turquoise*
7 *Light Turquoise*
8 *Deep Aqua*
9 *Purple*
10 *Blue*
11 *Yellow Green*
12 *Light Powder-Blue*
13 *Royal Blue*
14 Combine one strand *Deep Blue* with one strand *Blue*.
15 *Deep Blue*

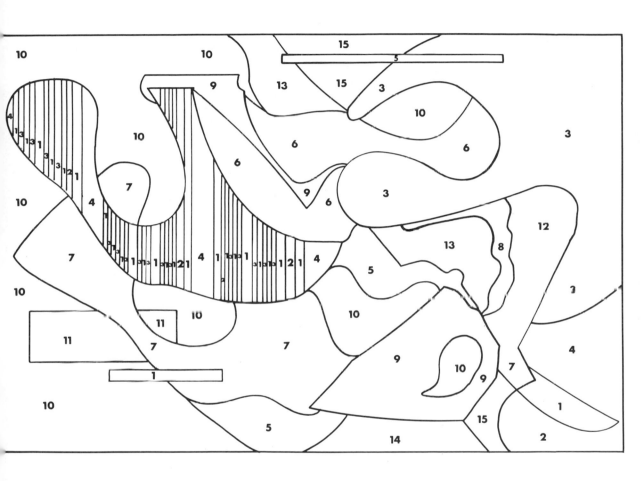

83

ARTICHOKE, GREEN PEAS, MUSHROOMS

MAGIC NEEDLE
Winnetka, Illinois

DESIGNER: *Miriam Krasno*

Color page 93.

All three pieces: 6" x 6" not including border; #12 mono canvas; 3-strand
Persian yarn split to 2 strands

These three small designs are ideal for kitchen decorations, either
mounted separately (see color page 93) or combined in one group-
ing (see drawing, page 85). Remember to stitch enough border so
that no blank canvas will show when the needlepoint is mounted.
Outline the design in continental and fill in with basketweave.

ARTICHOKE, GREEN PEAS, MUSHROOMS — *color key*

Artichoke
1   *Olive Green*
2   *Dark Green*
3   *Mint*

Green Peas
1   *Green*
2   *Chartreuse*
3   *Dark Green or Evergreen*
4   *Light Green*

Mushrooms
1   *Tan Ocher*
2   *Dark Brown*
3   *Ivory*
4   *Beige*

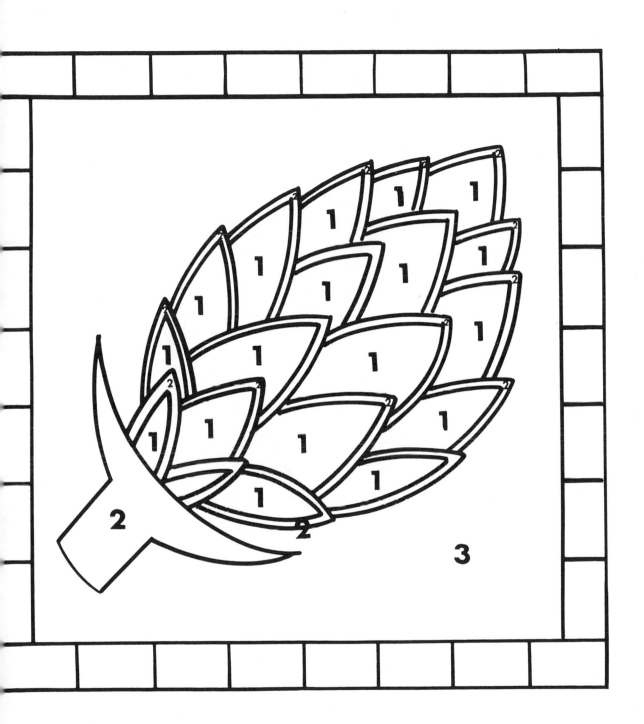

85

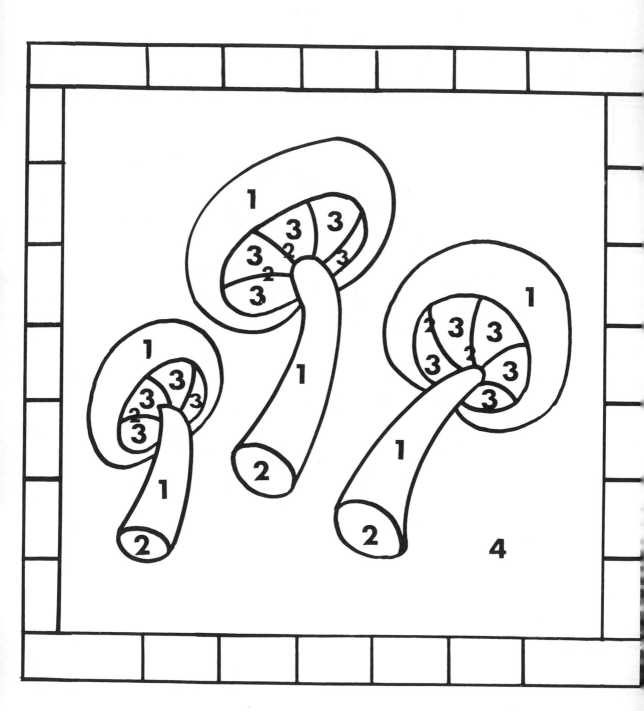

LEAF PILLOW

CUSTOM NEEDLEWORK STUDIO
Houston, Texas

DESIGNER: *Virginia Maxwell*

Color page 93.

12" x 18" overall; #10 mono canvas; 3-strand Persian yarn

This fun pillow is upholstered in a leaf shape. Because of the rather large mesh size, you may want to work the leaf area in one of the bargello stitches so that the butterfly, done in basketweave, will be delicate in contrast. Remember to stitch about one inch extra around the edge to allow for the irregular seam allowance in upholstering.

LEAF PILLOW — *color key*

1 *Olive Green*
2 *Dark Green or Evergreen*
3 *Dark Gray-Green*
4 *Burnt Umber*
5 *Brown*
6 *Cadmium Red*
7 *Citron*
8 *Chrome Orange*
9 *Aqua*
10 *Sea Blue*
11 *Cadmium Yellow*
12 *Shocking Pink*

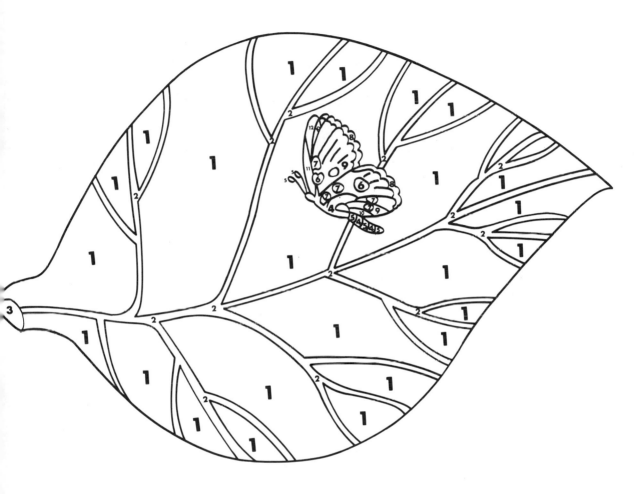

FROG ON A LILY PAD

THREADNEEDLE
Englewood, New Jersey

DESIGNER: *Louise Pitkin*

Color page 93.

10" x 10" overall dimensions; #14 mono canvas; 3-strand Persian yarn split to 2 strands

The canvas shown is done in continental and basketweave stitches, but it might be interesting if bargello stitches were used in the background. If this piece is to be mounted without a frame, allow enough border to fold over the edges on all sides.

FROG ON A LILY PAD — *color key*

1 *Cadmium Red*
2 *Dark Gray-Green*
3 *Deep Olive-Green*
4 *Yellow Green*
5 *Mint Green*
6 *White*
7 *Medium Gray-Green*

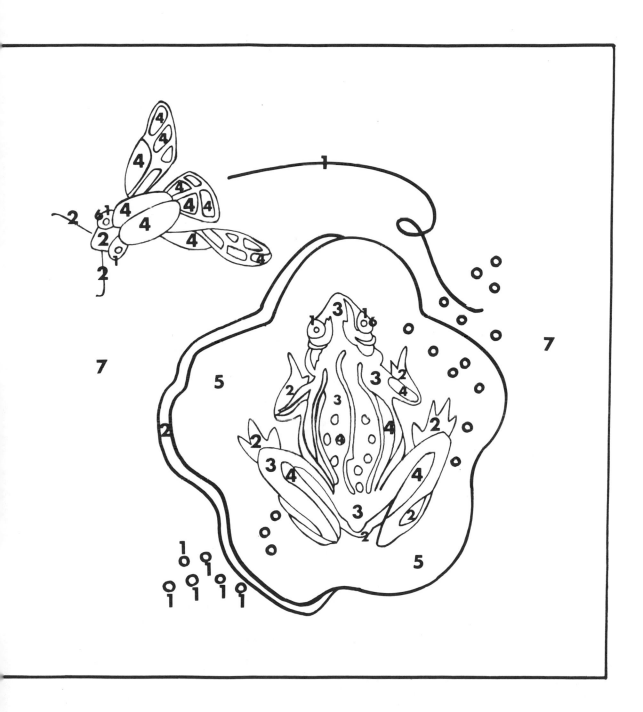

PLATE 13.

Opposite: Six Small Pieces: Artichoke, Green Peas, Mushrooms, page 84; Leaf Pillow, page 88; Frog on a Lily Pad, page 90; Owl Pillow, page 98

PLATE 14.

Overleaf: Sunburst, page 100

MOIRÉ

MUSEUM RECREATIONS, INC.
New York, New York

DESIGNERS: *Hilda Gabrilove, Nancy Koenigsberg*

Color page 112.

15″ x 15″; #14 mono canvas; 3-strand Persian yarn split to 2 strands

This design is unusual because, though a limited number of colors are used, a powerful sense of movement is achieved. The background may be executed in a variety of different colors, but remember that the color scheme should always be monochromatic. Use the simple basketweave stitch. Any attempt to use different stitches will destroy the movement achieved by the subtle use of color.

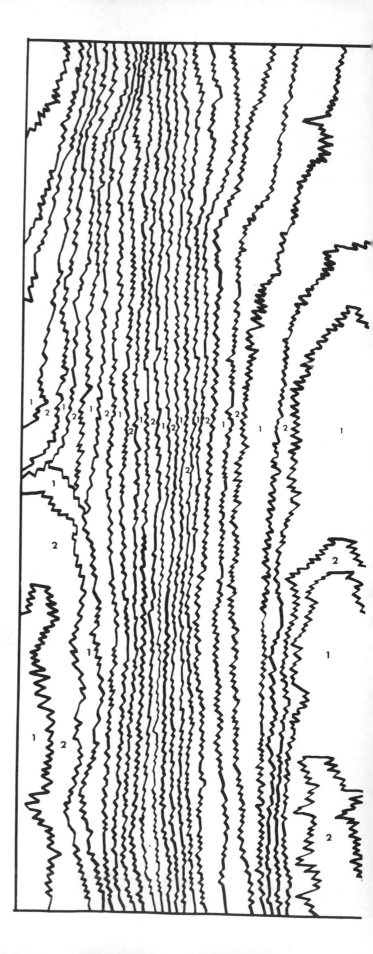

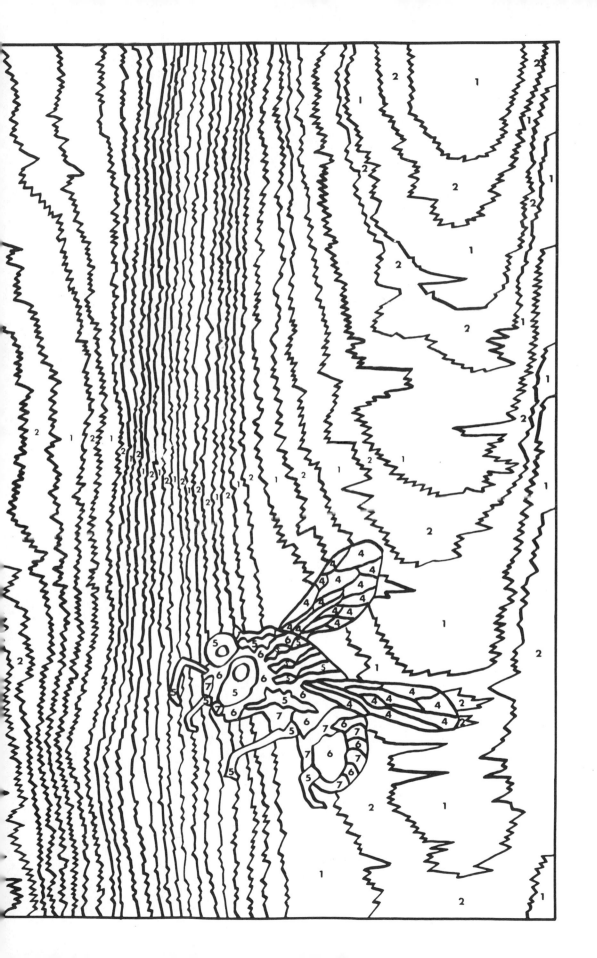

OWL PILLOW

NEEDLE IN A HAYSTACK
Dallas, Texas

DESIGNER: *Joyce Terrell*

Color page 93.

6" x 7" custom-shaped; #10 mono canvas; 3-strand Persian yarn, unsplit

This is a charming small throw pillow. It should be carefully upholstered because the design must be custom-shaped to the owl's body. Outline all areas in continental stitch and fill in with basketweave. You may want to add braided feet like those in the color picture, page 93.

OWL PILLOW — *color key*

1 *Light Wintergreen*
2 *Dark Wintergreen*
3 *Process Blue*
4 *Cadmium Yellow*
5 *Black*
6 *White*
7 *Ultra-Light Pale Yellow*

SUNBURST

DA NEEDLEPOINT
Far Rockaway, New York

DESIGNER: *Dennis M. Arnold*

Color page 94.

15" x 15" not including border; #12 mono canvas; 3-strand French or Persian yarn split to 2 strands

This design is shown in the square but can easily be worked in a round motif. Because of the many curved lines, read instructions for outlining curved areas, page 24. After outlining in continental, fill in with basketweave. A one-inch border should be allowed around the whole design for upholstering.

SUNBURST — *color key*

1 *Cadmium Orange*
2 *Cadmium Yellow*
3 *Life Red*
4 *Pale Yellow*
5 *Cream*
6 *Light Brown*
7 *Dark Yellow or Goldenrod*
8 *Chocolate Brown*
9 *Deep Dark-Brown*

101

ORIENTAL GOOD-LUCK SYMBOL

SIGN OF THE ARROW
St. Louis, Missouri

DESIGNER: *Penny Penning (Pennykins)*

Color page 111.

15"-diameter circle; #14 mono canvas; 3-strand Persian yarn split to 2 strands

This Oriental good-luck sign symbolizes health, wealth, and longevity. The design should be done in muted colors, using the basket-weave stitch or one of the many simple bargello stitches found in any good stitchery book (see Bibliography).

ORIENTAL GOOD-LUCK SYMBOL — *color key*

BACKGROUND:
1 *Avocado Green*

SYMBOL:
2 *Cadmium Yellow*

FISH:
3 *Salmon Orange*
4 *Black*

FLORAL SPLASH

NEEDLE IN A HAYSTACK
Dallas, Texas

DESIGNER: *Joyce Terrell*

Color page 137.

9" x 9" overall dimensions; #10 mono canvas; 3-strand Persian yarn

This simple floral design is easy to stitch and makes a handsome throw pillow. Outline all colored areas in continental stitch and fill in with basketweave. You may add the tassels to the corners as shown on color page 137 or leave a knife edge all around.

FLORAL SPLASH — *color key*

1   *Red Orange*
2   *Cadmium Orange*
3   *Yellow*
4   *Light Magenta or Shocking Pink*
5   *Deep Aqua*
6   *Green*
7   *Black*
8   *Pale Celery Green, Light*

CLASS INSTRUCTION PILLOW

THE OPEN DOOR TO STITCHERY
Great Neck, New York

DESIGNER: *The Open Door to Stitchery*

Color page 137.

14" x 16" overall dimensions; #12 mono canvas; 3-strand Persian yarn split to 2 strands

This is an ideal pattern for mastering many different kinds of stitches. Outline the "patches" in continental stitch, then work each area in any sequence, color, and stitch that suits your fancy. Suggested colors and stitches appear in the color list; see the Bibliography for a list of useful stitch-instruction books.

CLASS INSTRUCTION PILLOW — *color key*

FIRST ROW *(left to right)*
1 *Shocking Pink & White* (brick stitch)
2 *Dark Green, Pale Green, & Citron* (combining basketweave and bargello)
3 *White, Goldenrod, Cadmium Yellow, & Pale Yellow* (basketweave and bargello)
4 *Pale Pink & White* (Hungarian stitch)

SECOND ROW (left to right)
1 *Dark Green & White* (Florentine stitch)
2 *Pale Pink & White* (old mosiac)
3 *Goldenrod, Cadmium Yellow, & Pale Yellow* (Milanese stitch)
4 *Dark Green & White* (Kalem stitch)
5 *Dark Green, Pale Green, White, Light Pink, & Shocking Pink* (gobelin stitch)

THIRD ROW (left to right)
1 *Cadmium Yellow & Pale Yellow* (diagonal Scotch stitch and basketweave)
2 *Pale Green* (Parisian stitch)
3 *Shocking Pink & White* (Smyrna cross-stitch)
4 *Pale Green & White* (Byzantine stitch)

FOURTH ROW (left to right)
1 *Off-White* (cross-stitch)
2 *Dark Green, Pale Yellow, & White* (Byzantine stitch)
3 *Cadmium Yellow, Pale Pink, & White* (bargello stitch)
4 *Dark Green, Pale Green, & White* (basketweave stitch)

1	2	3	4

1	2	3	4	5

1	2	3	4

1	2	3	4

FIGURES & FLOWERS

CARDÉ LIMITED
Glenview, Illinois

DESIGNER: *Carole De Woskin*

Color page 138.

14" x 17" not including border; #12 mono canvas; 3-strand Persian yarn split to 2 strands

This design is perfect for a child's room. Soft pastel colors should be used for the background and vibrant colors should be used in the sunburst and clothing. Outline all colored areas in continental and fill in with basketweave.

FIGURES & FLOWERS — *color key*

1 *Goldenrod*
2 *Cadmium Orange*
3 *Black*
4 *White*
5 *Light Powder Blue*
6 *Chartreuse or Lime Green*
7 *Kelly Green*
8 *Flesh or Light Pink*
9 *Sky Blue*
10 *Shocking Pink*
11 *Magenta*
12 *Nubian Brown*

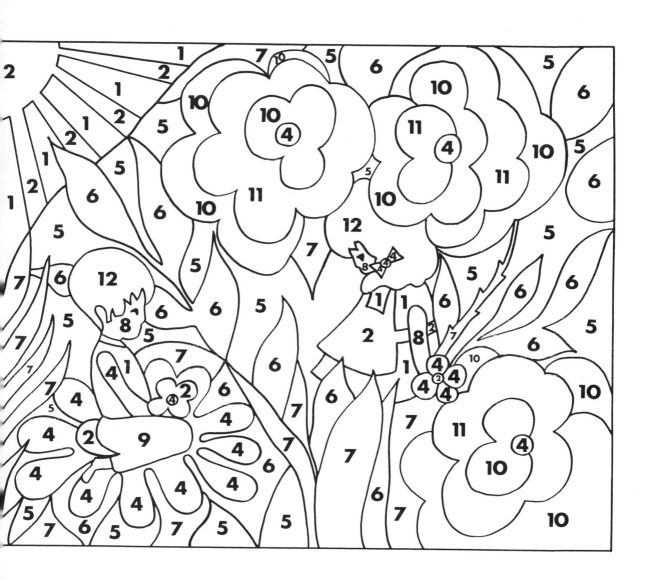

PLATE 15.
Opposite: Oriental Good-Luck Sign, page 102

PLATE 16.
Overleaf: Moiré, page 95

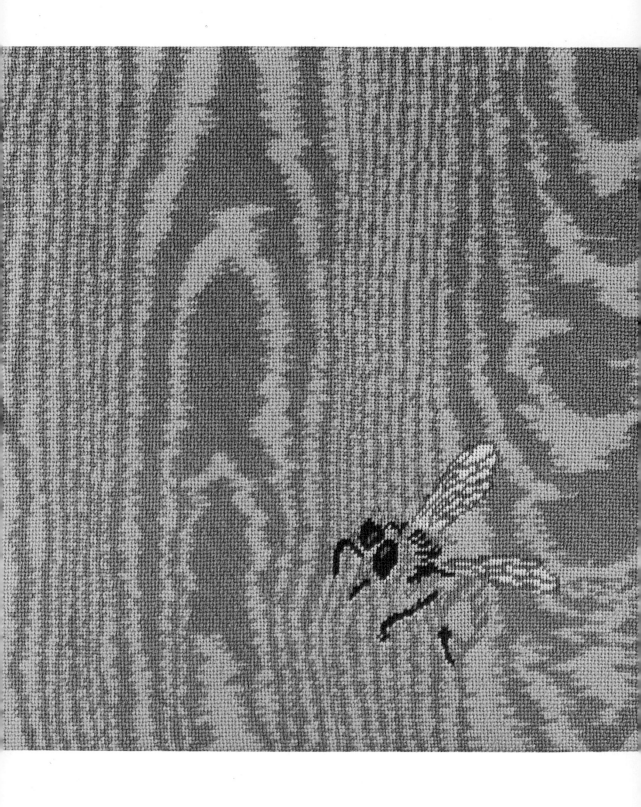

OPEN TULIPS

CREATIVE STITCHERY
Philadelphia, Pennsylvania

DESIGNER: *Creative Stitchery*

Color page 140.

14″ x 14″ overall; #10 mono canvas; 3-strand Persian yarn

This design appears intricate but is really simple, because all the areas that make up the shading are clearly outlined. There is no blending of one color into another. Outline each color with continental stitch and fill in with basketweave.

OPEN TULIPS—*color key*

1 *Pale White*
2 *Light Green*
3 *Dark Green*
4 *Cadmium Yellow*
5 *Magenta*
6 *Shocking Pink*
7 *Golden Orange*
8 *Light Brown*
9 *Light Rust*
10 *Deep Brown*

All heavy black lines on the tracing should be stitched in Number 3, *Dark Green*.

115

MINI BOY & MINI GIRL—JASON & ANDREA

SIGN OF THE ARROW
St. Louis, Missouri

DESIGNER: *Sign of the Arrow*

Color page 138.

3½" x 8½" overall dimensions; #14 mono canvas; 3-strand Persian yarn split to 2 strands

These little designs make up quickly and are ideal gifts for newborn babies. Outline the figures and the lettering in the name in continental stitch and fill in with basketweave. Work the background in any interesting bargello stitch.

MINI BOY & MINI GIRL — *color key*

MINI BOY (Jason)
1 *Brown*
2 *Flesh*
3 *Process Blue*
4 *White*
5 *Kelly Green*
6 *Chartreuse*
7 *Cadmium Yellow*
8 *Dark Brown*
9 *Pale Yellow*
10 *Life Red*

MINI GIRL (Andrea)
1 *Goldenrod*
2 *Pale Apricot*
3 *Blue*
4 *White*
5 *Chartreuse*
6 *Black*
7 *Life Red*
8 *Cadmium Yellow*

117

GERANIUMS

SANPIE, INC.
Lake Forest, Illinois

DESIGNER: *Patricia K. Ingersoll*

Color page 139.

13″ x 13″ overall dimensions; #10 mono canvas; 3-strand Paternayan Persian yarn

The impact of this design is achieved through a bold use of color. The variations of the magenta family combined with a subtle use of green create powerful movement throughout.

Outline the design in continental and fill in with basketweave. When stitching the border, remember to allow enough room for either upholstering or mounting. If you plan to change the color scheme, try to keep the flowers in bold colors and the background in muted tones.

GERANIUMS—*color key*

1 *Pale Pink*
2 *Shocking Pink or Bright Magenta*
3 *Cadmium Red*
4 *Deep Magenta*
5 *Deep Mint or Pale Kelly Green*
6 *Light Kelly Green*
7 *Grass Green*
8 *Kelly Green, Dark*
9 *Olive*

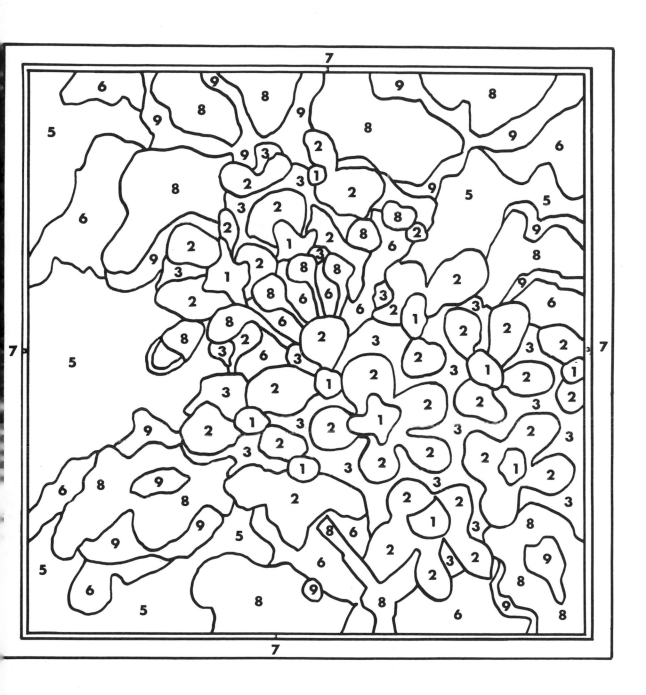

GRENOUILLE

NEEDLEPOINT U.S.A., INC.
New York, New York

DESIGNERS: *Cherie Neger, Elaine Oltarsh*

Color page 139.

10" x 14" overall dimensions, design custom-shaped; #12 mono canvas; 3-strand Persian yarn split to 2 strands

Trace the design onto the canvas and allow at least a half-inch seam allowance for upholstering. Work the design in basketweave, or you may experiment with a variety of stitches. This design will also work well in a variety of colors if you do not wish to follow those shown.

Upholster the underside of Grenouille in a plain fabric, picking up one of the colors in the needlepoint design, and stuff with Dacron or kapok. It is interesting to note that this frog can also be made into a beanbag as well as a pillow.

GRENOUILLE—*color key*

  1 *Aqua*
  2 *Deep Purple*
  3 *Deep Magenta*
  4 *Royal Blue*
  5 *Cadmium Yellow*
  6 *Ice Blue*
  7 *Cadmium Orange*
  8 *Deep Red*
  9 *Pale Pink*
 10 *Chartreuse*
 11 *Dark Green*
 12 *Light Blue*
 13 *White*

SAFARI BELT

ARROWPOINT
St. Louis, Missouri

DESIGNER: *Susan B. Rowe*

Color page 150.

$2\frac{1}{4}$" x 33"; #16 mono canvas; 3-strand English crewel yarn

Some may find this belt rather difficult to stitch. The main thing to keep in mind is that the canvas mesh size must be extremely small, or the fine detail in the animals will be lost.

Lengthwise, the finished belt must be equivalent to the waist measurement plus two inches to turn over to hold a clasp or enough additional length to accommodate the holes if you are making a prong-buckled belt. The best way to adjust the waist measurement is to add or subtract length at the grassy areas at the ends of the belt and between the animals.

Trace your pattern directly from the book. The width of the finished belt *can* vary, which is what happens if you use the photostating method of adjusting the pattern size. However, the pattern in this book is identical in size to the original belt and is recommended. If you make it much narrower, you will find the belt more difficult to stitch; and the change in size may destroy some of the beauty of the design.

Outline the animals in continental stitch. Fill in with basketweave.

SAFARI BELT — *color key*

1. Dark Gold
2. Golden Ocher
3. Gold
4. Burnt Umber
5. Dark Rust
6. Medium Rust
7. Light Rust
8. Black
9. White
10. Powder Blue

Grass colors are used at will between dark, medium, and light greens.

10

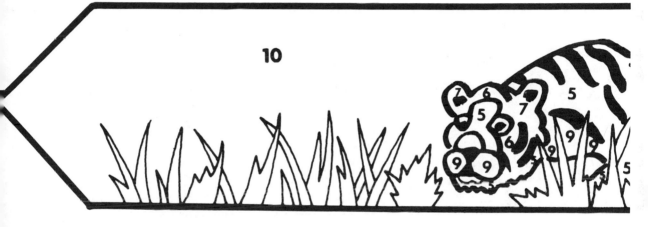

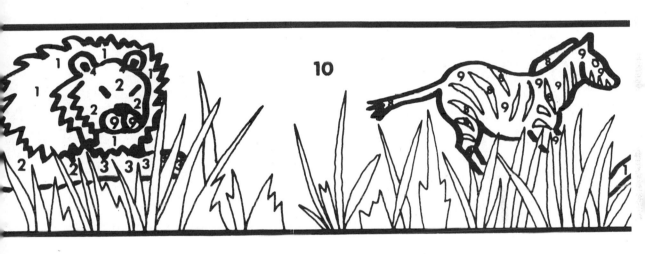

10

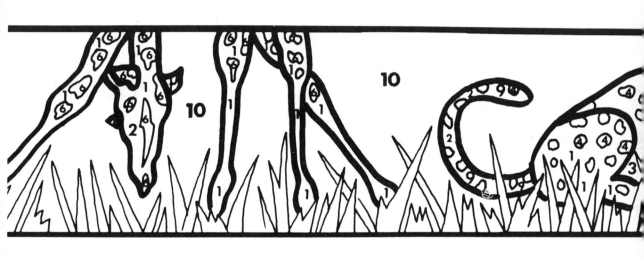

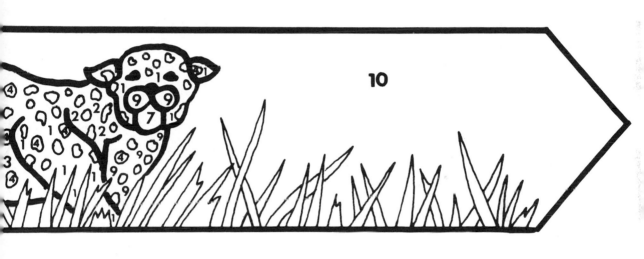

10

JUNGLE MOTIF

DA NEEDLEPOINT
Far Rockaway, New York

DESIGNER: *Dennis M. Arnold*

Color page 149.

14″ x 16″ not including border; #14 mono canvas; 3-strand Persian yarn split to 2 strands

Wild animals roam free amid exotic flowers and lush plants on this vivid, colorful pillow. Basketweave stitch should be used throughout because the design itself is extremely busy. If you wish to change the color scheme, remember to keep the colors bright—use no muted tones. A border may be stitched around the entire design to contain it.

JUNGLE MOTIF — *color key*

1 *Nile Green*
2 *Deep Cadmium Yellow*
3 *Deep Powder Blue*
4 *Pale Yellow or Deep Cream*
5 *Nubian Brown*
6 *Deep Brown*
7 *Deep Flesh*
8 *White*
9 *Chartreuse*
10 *Bright Tan*
11 *Pale Pink*
12 *Life Red*
13 *Shocking Pink*
14 *Deep Cadmium Red*
15 *Deepest Royal Green*
16 *Light Beige*
17 *Citron*
18 *Bright Magenta*
19 *Deep Rust-Brown*
20 *Deep Cool Gray*
21 *Process Blue*
22 *Peach*

129

GIRAFFE EYEGLASS CASE

PRISMS
St. Louis, Missouri

DESIGNER: *Priscilla Gunn*

Color page 149.

3" x 6" not including border; #18 mono canvas; 3-strand Persian yarn split to 1 strand

This unusual design makes an ideal gift. Combining the giraffe-skin pattern with a portrait of the animal is an exciting idea which may lead you to experiment with other wild animals and their skins. Work the entire design in basketweave and allow an extra row of needlepoint beyond the outline of the finished eyeglass case for upholstering. Measure the glasses that are to go into the case!

GIRAFFE EYEGLASS CASE — *color key*

1 *Dark Gold or Deep Ocher*
2 *Yellow Green*
3 *Black*
4 *Cream*
5 *Cadmium Red*
6 *White*

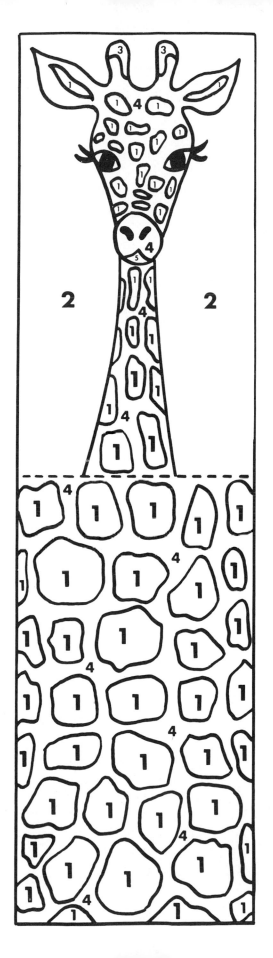

PATCHWORK TURTLE

NEEDLE IN A HAYSTACK
Dallas, Texas

DESIGNER: *Joyce Terrell*

Color page 138.

9" x 9" not including border; #10 mono canvas; 3-strand Persian yarn

This cute little patchwork turtle is ideal for a child's room and is an easy beginner's piece. Outline all colored areas in continental stitch and fill in with basketweave.

PATCHWORK TURTLE — *color key*

1 *Medium Green*
2 *Process Blue*
3 *Light Lime-Green*
4 *White*
5 *Magenta*
6 *Cadmium Orange*
7 *Cadmium Yellow*
8 *Black*
9 *Light Yellow-Green*

9

9

9

9

133

LOVE PILLOW

DEE NEEDLEPOINT ORIGINALS
Point Pleasant Beach, New Jersey

DESIGNER: *Dee Norton*

Color page 140.

14″ x 14″ overall dimensions; #12 mono canvas; 3-strand Persian yarn split to 2 strands

The combination of the colors with the lettering and the flower makes this a cheerful variation on the "Love" design. Each letter is done in a different bargello stitch with a slight variation in color. A list of the stitches used is found with the color list below. Remember to leave enough border for upholstering.

LOVE PILLOW — *color key*

1 *Light Olive-Green*
2 *Dark Olive-Green*
3 *Pale Golden-Yellow*
4 *Deep Reddish-Orange*
5 *Chrome Orange*
6 *Deep Brown or Black*
7 *Goldenrod*

STITCH CHART

A *Continental*
B *Bargello Byzantine*
C *Bargello Mosaic (Diagonal)*
D *Scotch Stitch*
E *Bargello Parisian*

134

135

BAMBOO

NEEDLEPOINT U.S.A., INC.
New York, New York

DESIGNERS: *Cherie Neger, Elaine Oltarsh*

Color page 150.

18½" x 13" overall dimensions; #12 mono canvas; 3-strand Persian yarn split to 2 strands

Animal-skin designs are most successful when they are as natural-looking as possible. Follow the color scheme closely. Outline the spots and the bamboo in continental, then fill in with basketweave.

BAMBOO — *color key*

1 *Black*
2 *Light Beige*
3 *Yellow Green*
4 *Off-White*

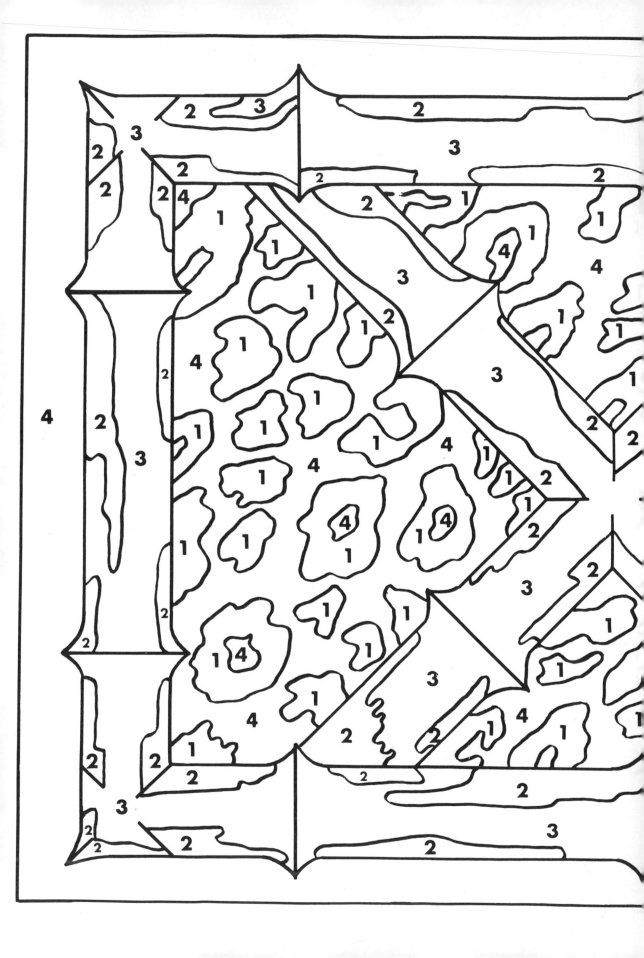

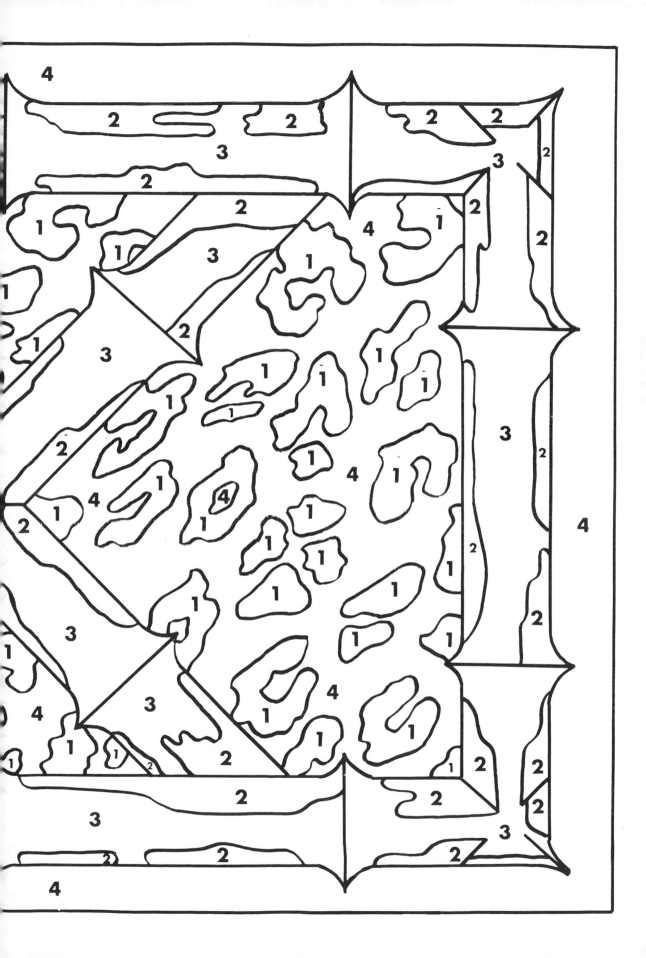

STRAWBERRIES

KNEEDLE-KNACK SHOP
Lahaska, Pennsylvania

DESIGNER: *Linda Gengarelly*

Color page 168.

13½" x 17" overall design; #10 mono canvas; 3-strand tapestry or Persian yarn, unsplit

This design works well as a pillow, wall hanging for the kitchen, or even a place mat covered with a piece of glass or Lucite. Outline the berries and work the black dots in continental stitch. Use basket-weave for filling in the berries and the background.

STRAWBERRIES — *color key*

1   *Black*
2   *Strawberry Red*
3   *Chartreuse*
4   *Dark Green*

STRAWBERRY PATCH

SIGN OF THE ARROW
St. Louis, Missouri

DESIGNER: *Mrs. Owen C. Goldwasser*

Color page 167.

11" x 13" overall pattern; #14 mono canvas; 3-strand Persian yarn split to 2 strands

Strawberry Patch, stitched with contrasting colors, makes a striking design. The deep navy-blue background makes the red strawberries almost jump off the surface of the pillow. If a navy-blue background is not suitable for your color scheme, any deep color will work well with this design. You may want to add a decoration to the center of the design.

Outline the design in continental stitch and fill in with basket-weave. The pillow shown is finished in a knife edge, but a boxed edge will work equally well. Remember to allow sufficient border for finishing.

STRAWBERRY PATCH — *color key*

1 *Cadmium Red*
2 *Light Olive*
3 *Navy Blue*
4 *Cream*
5 *Goldenrod or Deep Yellow*
6 *Deep Life Red*
7 *Olive*

147

PLATE 21.
Opposite: Giraffe Eyeglass Case, page 130; Jungle Motif, page 128

PLATE 22.
Overleaf: Safari Belt, page 122; Bamboo, page 141

148

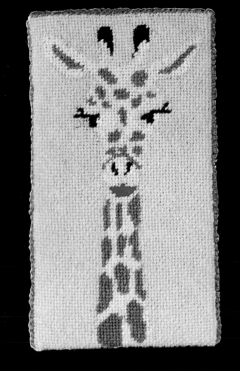
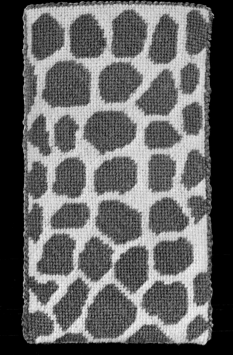

POPPY PURSE

ARROWPOINT
St. Louis, Missouri

DESIGNER: *Susan B. Rowe*

Color page 168.

9½" x 7¼" x 2¼" not including border; #14 mono canvas; 3-strand Persian yarn split to 2 strands

This is a detail from an Oriental design by Ketagawa Sosetsu, a seventeenth-century Japanese painter. The purse is stitched in basketweave in three separate parts, then stitched together to make up the bag. Needlepoint handbags are elegant, but they are expensive to have made up. Find an upholsterer and price the work before starting this design.

POPPY PURSE — *color key*

1 *Dark Green*
2 *Light Green*
3 *Cadmium Red*
4 *Vermilion*
5 *Pale Yellow*
6 *White*
7 *Process Blue*

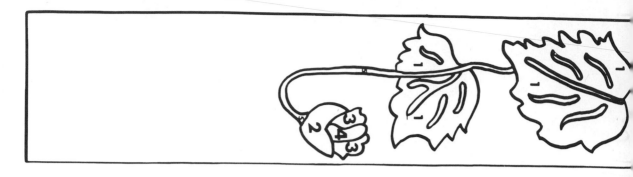

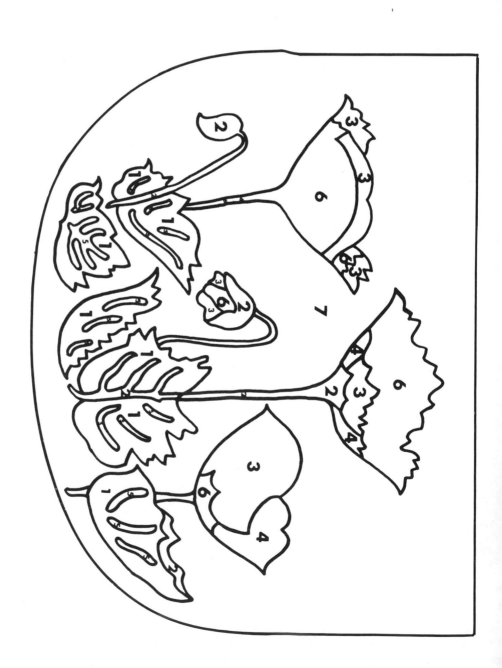

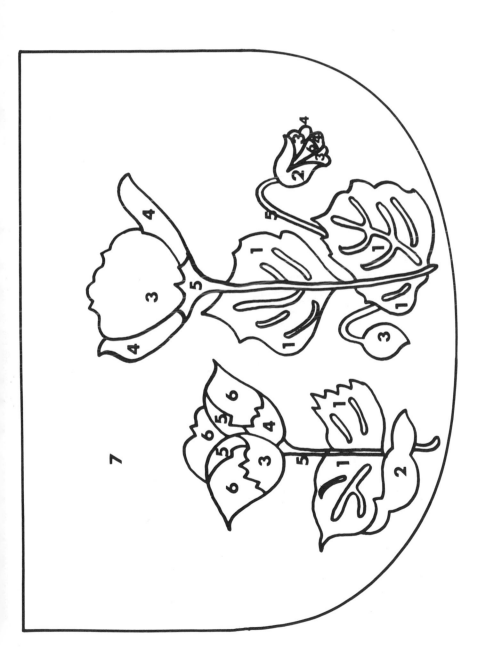

PATCHWORK PILLOW

NEEDLE IN A HAYSTACK
Dallas, Texas

DESIGNER: *Joyce Terrell*

Color page 168.

9" x 9" overall dimensions; #10 mono canvas; 3-strand Persian yarn, unsplit

This simple patchwork design may be the first steppingstone to creating your own patchwork designs. Outline each patch and each design within each patch in continental stitch. Fill in with basket-weave.

Feel free to change the color scheme, but keep the colors vivid. If you are an experienced needlepointer, try designing a more complicated border.

PATCHWORK PILLOW — *color key*

1 *Deep Kelly Green*
2 *Dark Green*
3 *Cadmium Red*
4 *Process Blue*
5 *Cadmium Yellow*
6 *Chrome Orange*
7 *Cadmium Orange*
8 *Deep Red-Orange*
9 *Bright Magenta*
10 *Deep Magenta*
11 *Chartreuse*
12 *White*
13 *Black*

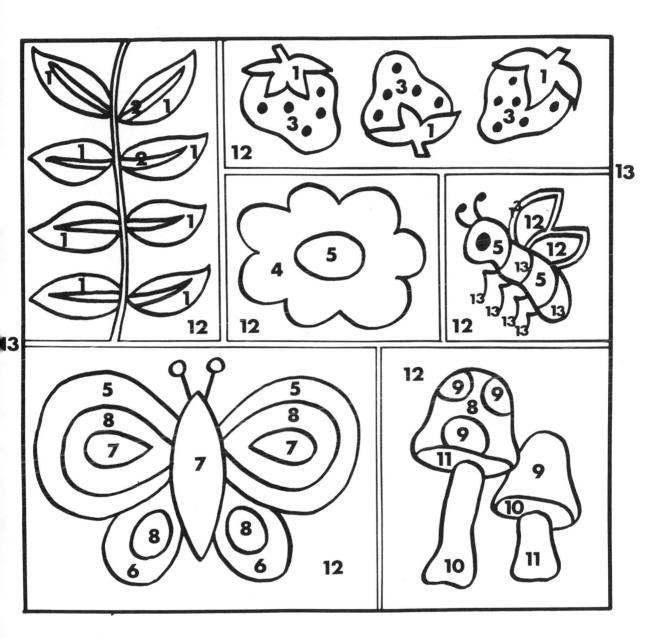

155

APPLE BELT

ARROWPOINT
St. Louis, Missouri

DESIGNER: *Susan B. Rowe*

Color page 167.

2″ plus waist size; #14 mono canvas; 3-strand Persian yarn split to 2 strands

To determine the length of the canvas, add the waist measurement plus two inches to hold the buckle; or if you are using a prong buckle, add extra length to accommodate the holes. Obtain your buckle before you begin working the needlepoint.

Outline the apples in continental and fill with basketweave. The color scheme may be altered to coordinate with your wardrobe.

APPLE BELT — *color key*

1. *Cadmium Red*
2. *Dark Green*
3. *Light Yellow-Green*
4. *Burnt Umber*
5. *Evergreen or Deep Green*

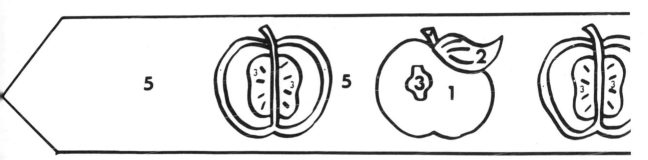

5

5

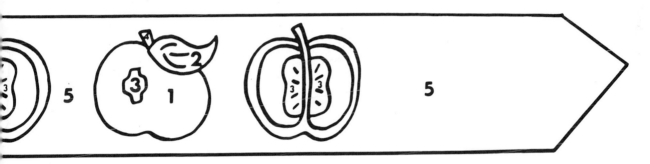

OUR KIDS PENCIL HOLDER

SIGN OF THE ARROW
St. Louis, Missouri

DESIGNER: *Nancy Near*

Color page 168.

4½" x 10" overall dimensions; #14 mono canvas; 3-strand Paternayan Persian yarn split to 2 strands

A needlepoint pencil holder is a great gift, and this design is perfect for a school-age child. Purchase an inexpensive pencil holder or make one yourself. Adjust the suggested dimensions of the canvas so that the needlepoint will cover the entire holder.

This design has been graphed for you, so simply follow the pattern, stitch for stitch, as it appears in the book (see "Stitch-for-Stitch Graphing," page 21). Outline the design in continental stitch and fill in with basketweave. Glue the finished canvas to the surface with Sobo glue, Elmer's glue, or a good upholstering paste.

OUR KIDS PENCIL HOLDER — *color key*

1. *Cadmium Yellow*
2. *Gold*
3. *Brown*
4. *Flesh*
5. *Process Blue*
6. *Nubian or Dark Brown*
7. *Shocking Pink*
8. *Dark Blue*
9. *Powder Blue*
10. *Black*
11. *Cadmium Red*

160

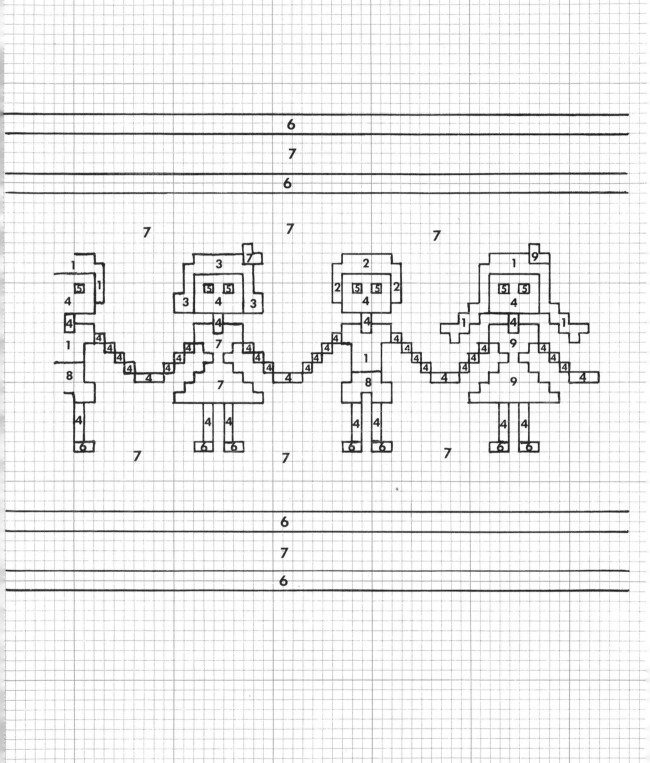

MOD NEEDLEPOINT-BY-THE-INCH BELT

PRISMS
St. Louis, Missouri

DESIGNER: *Priscilla Gunn*

Color page 168.

3" plus waist size; #10 mono canvas; 3-strand Persian yarn

This belt uses strong colors and string ties to achieve a very Mod effect. Use continental or basketweave stitches; or stitch the flowered areas in bargello. It is advisable to have the belt assembled professionally.

MOD NEEDLEPOINT-BY-THE-INCH BELT — *color key*

1 *White*
2 *Deep Cadmium Yellow*
3 *Bright Magenta*
4 *Deep Cadmium Red*
5 *Brilliant Life Red*
6 *Aqua*
7 *Process Blue*
8 *Royal Green*

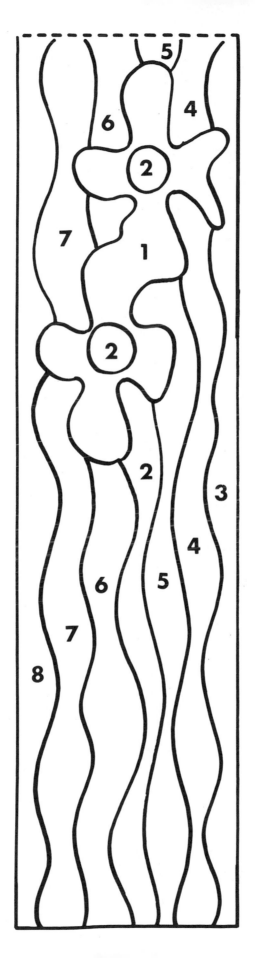

SANTA & TREE CHRISTMAS STOCKING

NEEDLE IN A HAYSTACK
Dallas, Texas

DESIGNER: *Joyce Terrell*

Color page 168.

18″ long; #10 mono canvas; 3-strand Paternayan Persian yarn

This Christmas stocking brings joy to any child year after year. Outline the design in continental stitch and fill in with basketweave. Block the finished needlepoint and back with red felt. Line it with red cotton. Bells can be sewn to the toe of the finished stocking.

SANTA & TREE CHRISTMAS STOCKING — *color key*

1 *Cadmium Red*
2 *Dark Red*
3 *Soft Pink*
4 *Warm Light-Gray*
5 *Black*
6 *White*
7 *Antique Gold*
8 *Brown*
9 *Kelly Green*
10 *Bright Lime-Green*
11 *Process Blue*
12 *Dark Blue*
13 *Cadmium Orange*
14 *Shocking Pink*
15 *Cadmium Yellow*
16 *Light Lime-Green*

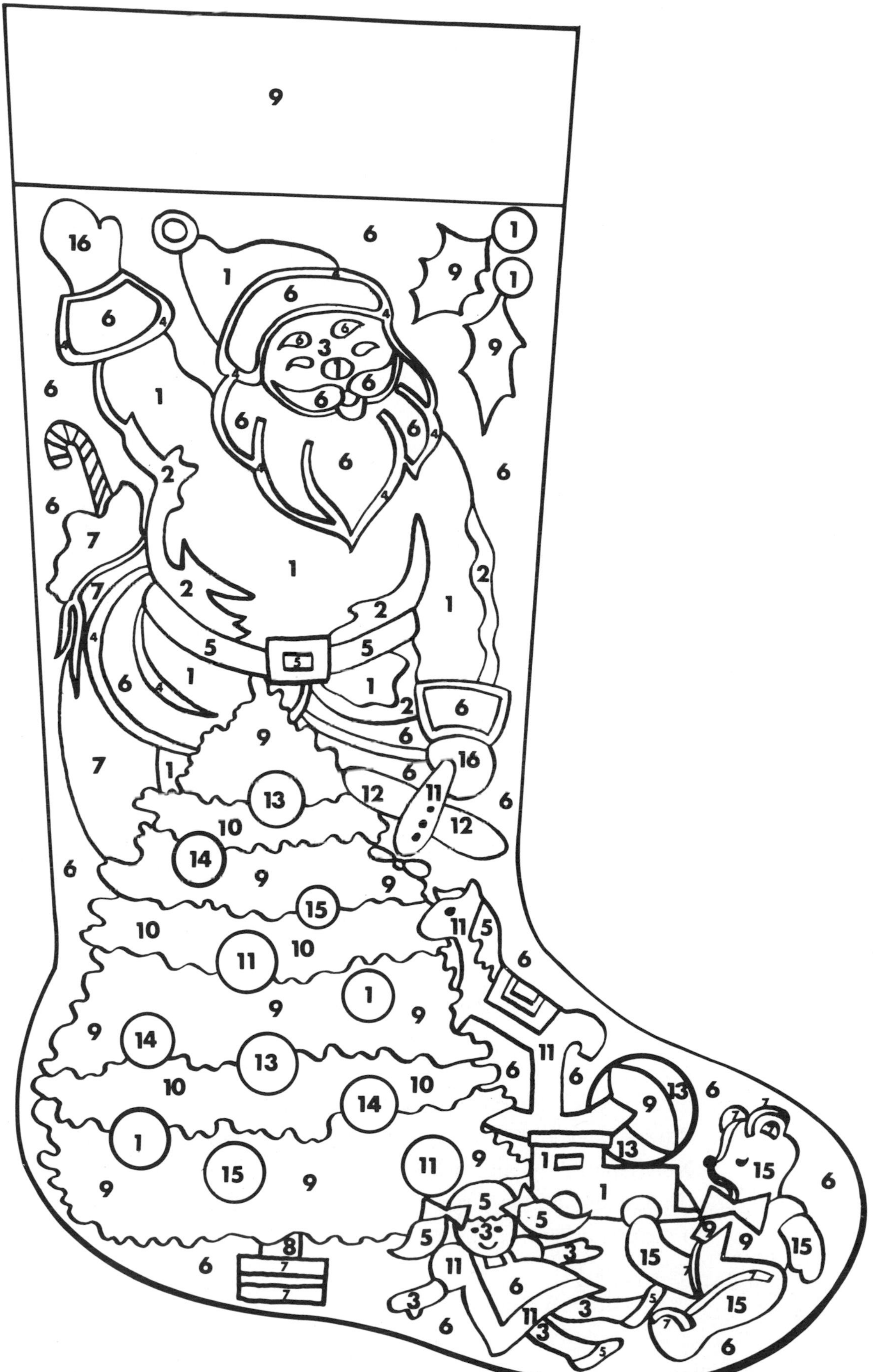

SANTA CLAUS & CHRISTMAS TREE ORNAMENTS

ARROWPOINT
St. Louis, Missouri

DESIGNER: *Susan B. Rowe*

Color page 168.

Santa Claus: 6½" x 3" overall dimensions; #14 mono canvas; 3-strand Persian yarn split to 2 strands

Christmas Tree: 5½" x 3½" overall dimensions; #14 mono canvas; 3-strand Persian yarn split to 2 strands

These little Christmas designs are easy, make up quickly, and bring joy year after year.

Outline the designs in continental stitch and fill in with basketweave. Cut out the designs allowing a half-inch of canvas all around the edge as seam allowance. Using a sewing machine, sew the back to the front, finished sides together, leaving the base open. Turn the ornament right side out, fill with kapok or Dacron stuffing, and close the opening with a blind stitch.

SANTA CLAUS & CHRISTMAS TREE ORNAMENTS — *color key*

SANTA CLAUS
1 *Cadmium Red*
2 *Dark Red*
3 *Shocking Pink*
4 *White*
5 *Light Beige or Tufted White*
6 *Gold*
7 *Black*
8 *Apple Green*

CHRISTMAS TREE
1 *Apple Green*
2 *Cadmium Red*
3 *Cadmium Yellow*
4 *Gold*
5 *Process Blue*
6 *Shocking Pink*

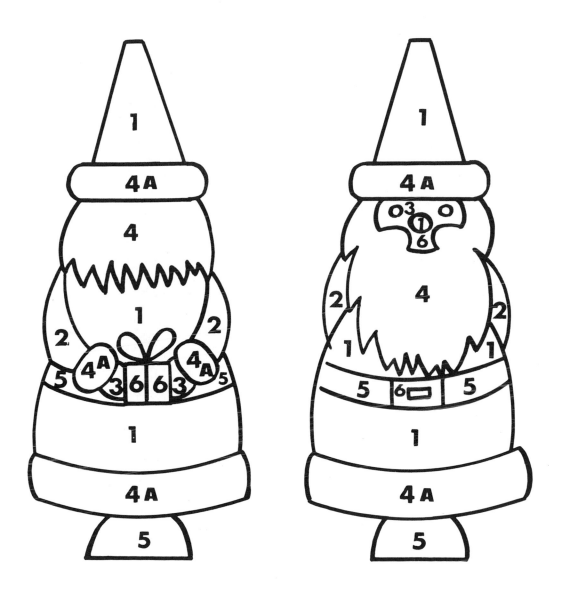

Shops and Designers

The following is a list of the shops and designers who contributed the pieces that appear in this book. Many of the shops sell their designs and materials by mail. Always be sure to write for a price list or catalog before submitting an order for specific materials.

AMERICAN CREWEL & CANVAS STUDIOS
P.O. Box 298
Boonton, New Jersey 07005

DESIGNER: *Nancy Rickert*

Designs may be obtained by writing directly to the shop. A catalog containing a listing of all needlepoint supplies and accessories carried by the shop is sent out three times a year to people on Stitch Witchery's mailing list.

ABSTRACT, color page 76.

ARROWPOINT
2200 Mueller Lane
St. Louis, Missouri 63131

DESIGNER: *Susan B. Rowe*

Arrowpoint is affiliated with Sign of the Arrow (see page 180) and is not a shop but a design source. All Arrowpoint designs may be purchased from the Sign of the Arrow. Custom designs and prepared needlepoint kits may be purchased by mail, but no accessories are available. A catalog is being planned.

SAFARI BELT, color page 150.
APPLE BELT, color page 167.
SANTA CLAUS & CHRISTMAS TREE ORNAMENTS, color page 168.
POPPY PURSE, color page 168.

CARDÉ LIMITED — SEW UNIQUE
246 Melba Lane
Highland Park, Illinois 60025

Cardé Limited is a design source and wholesale outlet. No mail order is available, but you may write to the shop for a listing of the stores where their designs can be purchased.

FIGURES & FLOWERS, color page 138.

NARCISSE CHAMBERLAIN

This designer has been the editor of several needlepoint books for William Morrow & Company, publishers of THE NEEDLEPOINT PATTERN BOOK. She does not design commercially.

OP BLOCKS INLAID IN 9 COLORS, color page 57.

CREATIVE STITCHERY
2116 Walnut Street
Philadelphia, Pennsylvania 19103

DESIGNERS: *Esther Kahn, Bluhma R. Silverman*

Creative Stitchery offers a complete mail-order line of canvas, wool, painted designs, needlepoint kits, books, and accessories. If custom designing is desired, the shop will both design the canvas and provide suggestions for stitching. Finished pieces may be sent for mounting.

TREE TOPS, color page 48.
OPEN TULIPS, color page 140.

CUSTOM NEEDLEWORK STUDIO
3404 Kirby Drive
Houston, Texas 77006

DESIGNER: *Virginia Maxwell*

Custom Needlework Studio carries wool, painted canvases, custom-ordered designs, needlepoint kits, books, and accessories. All items can be obtained by mail; write for a free brochure for precise listings and prices. If wool or canvas samples are requested, a small charge is made.

LEAF PILLOW, color page 93.

DA NEEDLEPOINT
1261 Central Avenue
Suite 711
Far Rockaway, New York 11691

DESIGNER: *Dennis M. Arnold*

No mail order is available directly from Mr. Arnold, but the department stores that carry his designs (Lord & Taylor, Bonwit Teller, Gimbel's, I. Magnin) will accept orders by mail. Mr. Arnold does custom designing; contact him at his studio.

OWL, color page 45.
SUNBURST, color page 94.
JUNGLE MOTIF, color page 149.

176

DEE NEEDLEPOINT ORIGINALS
P.O. Box 1756
Point Pleasant Beach, New Jersey 08742

DESIGNER: *Dee Norton*

Mail-order requests should be sent directly to the shop. Write for a series of catalogs and brochures explaining available designs. The shop carries a full line of wool, painted canvas designs, and prepared kits. Custom designs can be ordered, and requests for mounting of finished designs will also be handled.

CAPTAIN'S HAT, color page 35.
LOBSTER, color page 35.
MOUSE WITH NEEDLE, color page 36.
LOVE PILLOW, color page 140.

KNEEDLE-KNACK SHOP
Peddlers Village
Lahaska, Pennsylvania 18931

DESIGNER: *Linda Gengarelly*

The Kneedle-Knack Shop has no catalog; however, canvas, wool, and other needlepoint accessories are available by mail. Write to the shop for price information. Samples are available for a small charge, and custom designing is done upon request.

STRAWBERRIES, color page 168.

MAGIC NEEDLE
44 Green Bay Road
Winnetka, Illinois 60093

DESIGNER: *Miriam Krasno*

Ask for price of the Magic Needle's mail-order catalog. The shop carries prepared painted canvases and needlepoint kits, and will also prepare custom designs. Finished canvases may be sent for mounting.

ARTICHOKE, GREEN PEAS, MUSHROOMS, color page 93.

MUSEUM RECREATIONS, INC.
220 East 57th Street
Suite 2B
New York, New York 10022

DESIGNERS: *Hilda Gabrilove, Nancy Koenigsberg*

Museum ReCreations has a limited mail-order business, but no brochure, price list, or catalog is available. Custom designs may be ordered by mail, and requests must include a sketch or photograph and wool swatches. Museum ReCreations sells blank canvas, prepared painted designs, wool, and some accessories. They will also take finished needlepoint for mounting or pillow upholstering. Write or telephone the shop for information.

MOIRÉ, color page 112.

NEEDLE IN A HAYSTACK
5500 Greenville Avenue
Suite 216
Dallas, Texas 75206

DESIGNER: *Joyce Terrell*

Needle in a Haystack does not have a brochure or catalog, so requests must be made by letter to the shop. There is a small charge for wool, canvas samples, or pictures of designs. The shop carries blank canvas, wool, prepared designs and kits, and books on needlepoint. Finished canvases may be sent for mounting to: Needlepoint Finishing, Inc., 6615 Snider Plaza, Dallas, Texas 75205.

WATERMELON WEDGE, color page 17.
GOLD MEDALLION (SCROLL WALL HANGING), color page 58.
BUTTERFLY REPEAT PATTERN, color page 75.
OWL PILLOW, color page 98.
FLORAL SPLASH, color page 137.
PATCHWORK TURTLE, color page 138.
PATCHWORK PILLOW, color page 168.
SANTA & TREE CHRISTMAS STOCKING, color page 168.

NEEDLEPOINT U.S.A., INC.
37 West 57th Street
New York, New York 10019

DESIGNERS: *Cherie Neger, Elaine Oltarsh*

Designs and information may be obtained by mail. A small charge is made for catalogs listing all designs and supplies. This is basically a wholesale design house, so many of its designs can be found at leading department stores and specialty shops throughout the country.

GRENOUILLE, color page 139.
BAMBOO, color page 150.

NEEDLEPOINT DESIGN
Bergdorf Goodman
754 Fifth Avenue
New York, New York 10019

312 Worth Avenue
Palm Beach, Florida 33480

DESIGNER: *Lou Gartner*

No mail orders are accepted at either store. Both shops carry a constantly changing stock of prepared needlepoint designs and kits. Mr. Gartner will personally arrange by correspondence with you or with your decorator for custom designs. He specializes in rugs.

PAISLEY PILLOW—LIGHT AGAINST DARK, color page 18.

NEEDLEPOINT, INC.
2401 Magazine Street
New Orleans, Louisiana 70130

DESIGNER: *J. Wilson Raker*

A mail-order catalog is available for a small charge, listing all designs, canvas types, wool, and other needlepoint accessories. Custom orders are available on request, and finished designs may be sent for mounting if the original canvas was purchased from the shop.

PINEAPPLE MOTIF, color page 75.

THE OPEN DOOR TO STITCHERY
4 Bond Street
Great Neck, New York

DESIGNER: *The Open Door to Stitchery*

The Open Door to Stitchery is a charitable organization; all proceeds· go to the Foundation for Emotionally Disturbed Children, and the staff is made up entirely of volunteers donating their time and skills. The shop carries a complete line of DMC wools, canvas, and commercial designs. Custom designing is done on request. Write to the shop for specific information.

ORIENTAL RECTANGLE, color page 58.
CLASS INSTRUCTION PILLOW, color page 106.

PRISMS
9401 Sonora Avenue
St. Louis, Missouri 62144

DESIGNER: *Priscilla Gunn*

Prisms sells prepared painted designs and kits by mail. A catalog is available for a small charge, or you may write directly to the shop for additional information. Custom designing can be done to your specifications. All Prisms designs and needlepoint kits may be found at Sign of the Arrow (see page 180).

GIRAFFE EYEGLASS CASE, color page 149.
MOD NEEDLEPOINT-BY-THE-INCH BELT, color page 168.

ROBIN HOOD WOOL SHOP
P.O. Box 534
336 College Avenue
Clemson, South Carolina 29631

DESIGNER: *Marion E. Scoular*

The Robin Hood Wool Shop sells by mail, but no catalog is available at the present time. The shop carries canvas in all sizes, a complete line of wool yarns, and wide selection of needlepoint books. Its specialty is charting bargello designs. Finished pieces may be sent for blocking but not for mounting.

BLOCK DESIGN (CLEMSON), color page 48.

SANPIE, INC.
179 East Deerpath Avenue
Lake Forest, Illinois 60045
DESIGNER: *Patricia K. Ingersoll*

A mail-order catalog is available for a nominal charge, listing all designs and supplies that the shop carries—canvas in all sizes, a complete line of Paternayan yarns, and all needlepoint accessories. Finished designs may be sent for mounting or upholstering. The shop will be glad to do custom designing of any nature.

GERANIUMS, color page 139.

SIGN OF THE ARROW
9666 Clayton Road
St. Louis, Missouri 63124

DESIGNERS: *Nancy Near, Penny Pennings (Pennykins), Mrs. Owen C. Goldwasser, Linde Wiedow*

Sign of the Arrow is a nonprofit organization affiliated with Arrowpoint (see page 175), which donates all its proceeds to Arrowmont, a craft school in Gatlinburg, Tennessee, and to Care and Counciling, a St. Louis mental-health service for troubled families.

Sign of the Arrow sells canvas, wools, painted designs, custom-ordered designs, and needlepoint books by mail. You can obtain a catalog listing prices by writing to the shop. Mounting services are provided for St. Louis customers only.

MOD MONOGRAMS, color page 76.
ORIENTAL GOOD-LUCK SYMBOL, color page 111.
MINI BOY & MINI GIRL, color page 138.
STRAWBERRY PATCH, color page 167.
OUR KIDS PENCIL HOLDER, color page 168.

SOOKIE SOLON DESIGNS
420 East 72nd Street
New York, New York 10021

DESIGNER: *Sookie Solon*

Mail order is available for custom designs only. Any design appearing in this book may be ordered in kit form, and custom designs are available as long as all measurements and color requirements are included. This is strictly a design house and no needlepoint supplies or accessories are sold.

KNOCKOUT SCENE, color page 46.
FAIRY TALE SCENE, color page 46.
AMANDA, color page 47.

THREADNEEDLE
7 East Palisade
Englewood, New Jersey 07631

DESIGNERS: *Louise Pitkin, Doris Gerald*

Prepared designs and custom designs may be obtained by mail from Threadneedle. You may obtain a catalog for a small charge by writing directly to the shop. In addition to a complete line of needlepoint supplies, the shop also carries such accessories as belt buckles, footstools, luggage racks, and director's chairs. Finished canvases may be sent to the shop for mounting.

FROG ON A LILY PAD, color page 93.

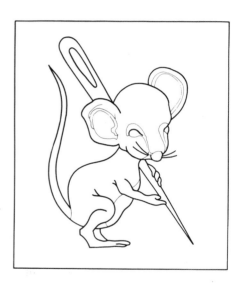

BIBLIOGRAPHY

Gartner, Louis J., Jr., NEEDLEPOINT DESIGN. New York, William Morrow & Company, 1970.

Gladstone, Meredith & Gary, THE NEEDLEPOINT ALPHABET BOOK. New York, William Morrow & Company, 1973.

Hammond, Natalie Hays, NEW ADVENTURES IN NEEDLEPOINT DESIGN. New York, Simon & Schuster, 1973.

Hanley, Hope, NEEDLEPOINT. New York, Charles Scribner's Sons, 1964.

Hanley, Hope, NEEDLEPOINT IN AMERICA. New York, Charles Scribner's Sons, 1969.

Hanley, Hope, NEW METHODS IN NEEDLEPOINT. New York, Charles Scribner's Sons, 1966.

Ireys, Katharine, FINISHING & MOUNTING YOUR NEEDLEPOINT. New York, Thomas Y. Crowell, 1973.

Kaestner, Dorothy, FOUR WAY BARGELLO. New York, Charles Scribner's Sons, 1972.

Lane, Maggie, MORE NEEDLEPOINT BY DESIGN. New York, Charles Scribner's Sons, 1972.

Lane, Maggie, NEEDLEPOINT BY DESIGN. New York, Charles Scribner's Sons, 1970.

Perrone, Lisbeth, THE NEW WORLD OF NEEDLEPOINT: *101 Exciting Designs in Bargello, Quickpoint, Grospoint & Other Repeat Patterns.* New York, Random House, 1972.

Picken, Mary B., & White, Doris, NEEDLEPOINT FOR EVERYONE. New York, Harper & Row, 1970.

Picken, Mary B., & White, Doris. NEEDLEPOINT MADE EASY. New York, Harper & Row, 1955.

Swain, Margaret H., DEVOTIONAL MISCELLANY. New York, The New York Graphics Society, 1966.

Wilson, Erica, ERICA WILSON'S EMBROIDERY BOOK. New York, Charles Scribner's Sons, 1973.

Williams, Elsa, BARGELLO EMBROIDERY. New York, Van Nostrand Reinhold, 1967.

JOSEPH MIDTHUN   SAMUEL HITI

BUILDING BLOCKS OF MATHEMATICS

DIVISION

WORLD
BOOK

a Scott Fetzer company
Chicago
www.worldbook.com

World Book, Inc.
233 N. Michigan Avenue
Chicago, IL 60601
U.S.A.

For information about other World Book publications,
visit our website at www.worldbook.com
or call 1-800-WORLDBK (967-5325).
For information about sales to schools and libraries,
call 1-800-975-3250 (United States),
or 1-800-837-5365 (Canada).

Library of Congress Cataloging-in-Publication Data

Division.
    pages cm. -- (Building blocks of mathematics)
  Summary: "A graphic nonfiction volume that
introduces critical division concepts"-- Provided by
publisher.
  Includes index.
  ISBN 978-0-7166-1433-3 -- ISBN 978-0-7166-1474-6
(pbk.)
  1. Division--Comic books, strips, etc.--Juvenile
literature. 2. Graphic novels. I. World Book, Inc.
QA115.D575 2013
513.2'14--dc23
                        2012031042

Building Blocks of Mathematics
ISBN: 978-0-7166-1431-9 (set, hc.)

Printed in the United States of America by
Worzalla, Stevens Point, WI
1st printing December 2012

Acknowledgments:
Created by Samuel Hiti and Joseph Midthun
Art by Samuel Hiti
Written by Joseph Midthun
Special thanks to Anita Wager, Hala
Ghousseini, and Syril McNally.

TABLE OF CONTENTS

THREE'S COMPANY
Hey Addition!
Hey Multiplication!
What are you up to?
Well, we found some sea shells!
A total of 9!
We are trying to split them up between us!
But we can't figure out how to do it equally!
Why don't I lend you a hand?
Would you?!
We could split the shells between the 3 of us!
That's fine with me as long as we split them equally!
Easy! I would write 9 divided by 3 like this:
9 ÷ 3 = ?
Let's try counting the shells into equal groups of 3 until we run out.
Great idea!
Scoop

7

8

We fit 3 balls in each bag!

So, now the balls are divided equally among the bags!

WOO-HOO!

See how we divided 12 evenly into 4 groups of 3?

If we wrote it as an equation, it would look like this:

$$12 \div 4 = 3$$

HEADS UP!

GOOOOAAAL!

Now, that's what I call teamwork!

BONK

CHIP

ROCKS IN BOXES

Have you ever seen my rock collection?

No!

I have 15 agates...

Cool!

Psst!

Agates is pronounced "AG-ihts."

Whenever I'm finished looking at my agates, I put them in special boxes to keep them safe.

Each box holds 5 rocks.

So, how many boxes do you need in all?

Hmm.

I can help!

We just need to find out how many groups of 5 are in 15.

Let's write it out like this:

We can solve this by separating the rocks into sets of 5.

I'm in!

I can help, too.

PLOP

5!

10!

15!

There are 3 groups of 5!

So, you need 3 boxes to hold all the rocks!

I knew that...

ZIP

We can walk 3 kilometers in 1 hour.

We use kilometers to measure distance.

If we continue on at this pace, how many hours will it take us to walk a distance of 18 kilometers?

We can write the problem as an equation, like this...

$$18 \div 3 = ?$$

Can we use a number line to help?

Let's count up by 3 kilometers, or *km*!

Sure!

3 km!

6 km!

9 km!

12 km!

15 km!

That's 1 hour!

2 hours.

3 hours.

4 hours.

5 hours.

We're close...

3   6   9   12   15

CAMPING OUT
I packed 28 graham crackers for all of us to share!
My absolute favorite!
I separated the crackers into 4 baggies, so that we each get the same amount.
How much is that?

Well, let's see if you three can figure it out!
Counting out 28 into 4 groups would take a while.
Yeah, and I'm hungry!
Yeah.

Good thing I know how we can solve this problem *fast*!
Follow me!
Boing
PLOP

Watch!
We can split 28 in half to make the solution easier to see!
I see 2 groups of 14!
squeak

Good eye!
We can also divide each group of 14 into 2 groups.
Four groups of 7!
That's 7 crackers each!
28
14 14
7 7 7 7

DIVISION IN THE WILD
Look–a grizzly bear in its natural habitat!
Wow!
splash
splash

If that bear catches exactly 7 salmon an hour...
...how many hours will it take the bear to catch 35 fish altogether?

We can use division to find out!

$$35 \div 7 = ?$$

We need to find out how many groups of 7 are in 35. That will tell us how many hours it will take!

Why not count up by 7's on a number line?

Munch!
Munch!
Munch!
Munch!
Munch!

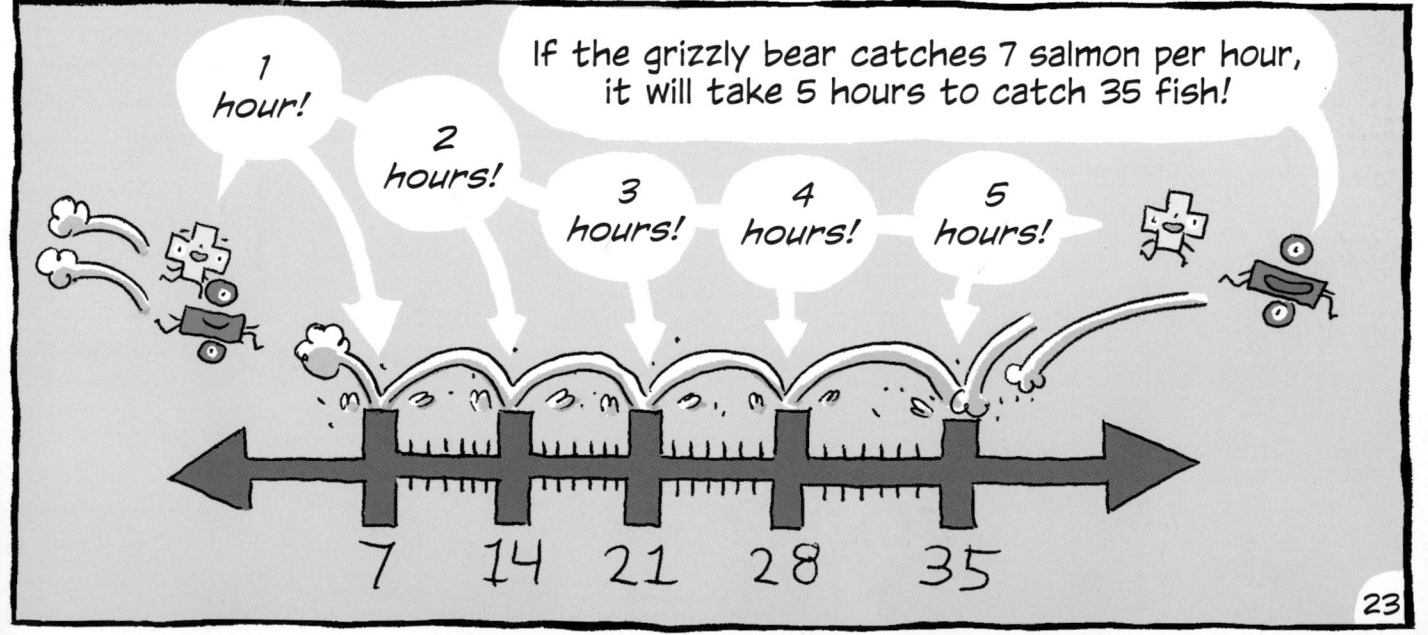

1 hour!

2 hours!

3 hours!

4 hours!

5 hours!

If the grizzly bear catches 7 salmon per hour, it will take 5 hours to catch 35 fish!

7   14   21   28   35

It seems as though this bear has stored up a little extra fat for the winter.
You'd better believe it!
Actually, I've gained 21 kilograms over the past 3 weeks.
Kilograms are a measurement of weight!
If the bear gained the same amount of weight each week, how much did it gain in just 1 week?
Write it like this:
21 ÷ 3 = ?
We need to divide 21 into 3 groups. Each group represents 1 week.
Let's use 5-kilogram weights!
PLOP

I know a way that we could check your work!

Shh!

Z.

Sorry.

We can use the multiplication facts we already know...

How do you mean?

Well, we know that 6 x 3 = 18.

That's 6 groups of 3...

Hmm.

So, we can start at 18 and count up to find out how many more groups of 3 are in 21.

Show us on a number line.

Okay.

26

At 18, we are only 3 away from 21.

That's 1 more group of 3...

0   18 19 20 21

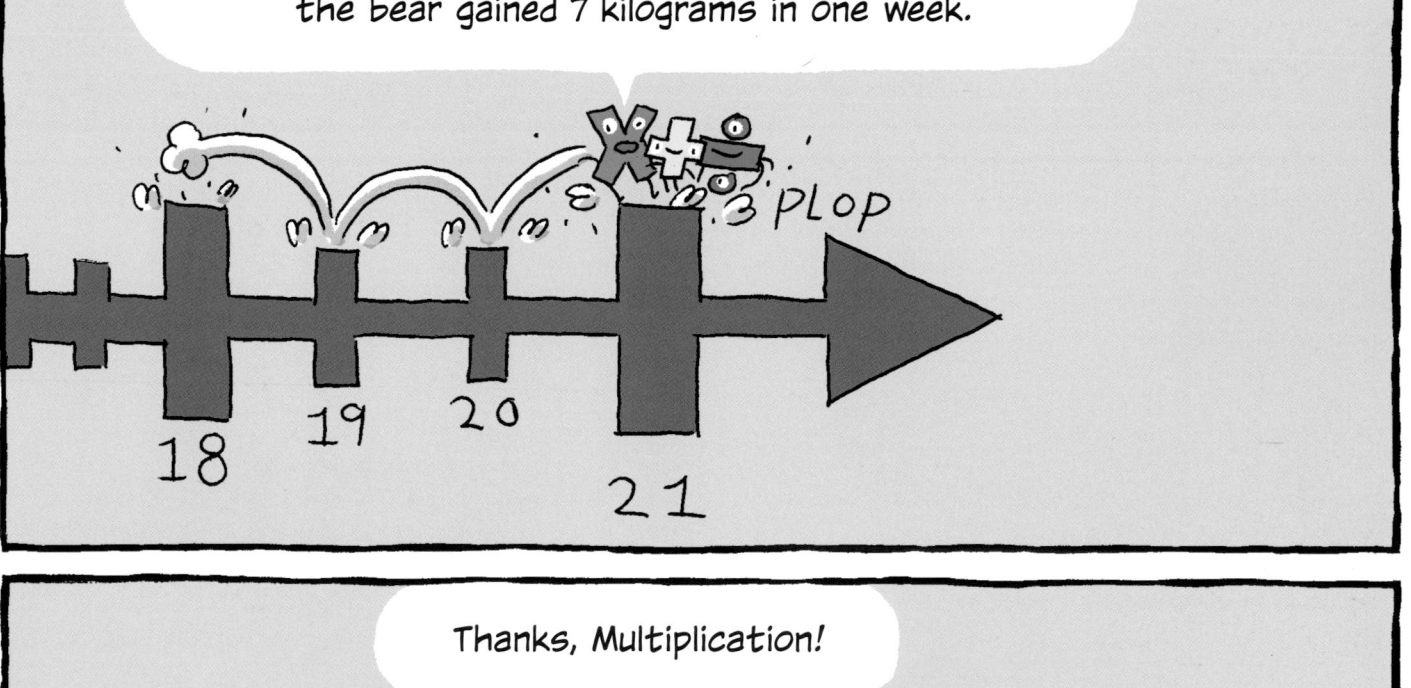

...for a total of 7 groups. So your answer was right— the bear gained 7 kilograms in one week.

18   19   20   21   PLOP

Thanks, Multiplication!

DIVISION FACTS

This table can help you multiply and divide fast!
It can also start you on your way to learning your division fact families.
A fact family shows how groups of numbers are related.

The table shows 10 different fact families for multiplication
and division. Can you think of more fact families?

1 x 1 = 1 1 ÷ 1 = 1	2 x 1 = 2 2 ÷ 1 = 2 2 ÷ 2 = 1	3 x 1 = 3 3 ÷ 1 = 3 3 ÷ 3 = 1	4 x 1 = 4 4 ÷ 1 = 4 4 ÷ 4 = 1	5 x 1 = 5 5 ÷ 1 = 5 5 ÷ 5 = 1
1 x 2 = 2 2 ÷ 2 = 1 2 ÷ 1 = 2	2 x 2 = 4 4 ÷ 2 = 2	3 x 2 = 6 6 ÷ 2 = 3 6 ÷ 3 = 2	4 x 2 = 8 8 ÷ 2 = 4 8 ÷ 4 = 2	5 x 2 = 10 10 ÷ 2 = 5 10 ÷ 5 = 2
1 x 3 = 3 3 ÷ 3 = 1 3 ÷ 1 = 3	2 x 3 = 6 6 ÷ 3 = 2 6 ÷ 2 = 3	3 x 3 = 9 9 ÷ 3 = 3	4 x 3 = 12 12 ÷ 3 = 4 12 ÷ 4 = 3	5 x 3 = 15 15 ÷ 3 = 5 15 ÷ 5 = 3
1 x 4 = 4 4 ÷ 1 = 4 4 ÷ 4 = 1	2 x 4 = 8 8 ÷ 4 = 2 8 ÷ 2 = 4	3 x 4 = 12 12 ÷ 4 = 3 12 ÷ 3 = 4	4 x 4 = 16 16 ÷ 4 = 4	5 x 4 = 20 20 ÷ 4 = 5 20 ÷ 5 = 4
1 x 5 = 5 5 ÷ 1 = 5 5 ÷ 5 = 1	2 x 5 = 10 10 ÷ 5 = 2 10 ÷ 2 = 5	3 x 5 = 15 15 ÷ 5 = 3 15 ÷ 3 = 5	4 x 5 = 20 20 ÷ 5 = 4 20 ÷ 4 = 5	5 x 5 = 25 25 ÷ 5 = 5

FIND OUT MORE

BOOKS

Cheetah Math: Learning About Division from Baby Cheetahs
by Ann Whitehead Nagda
(Henry Holt, 2007)

Divide and Ride
by Stuart J. Murphy
(HarperCollins Publishers, 1997)

Divide It Up
by Tonya Leslie and Ari Ginsburg
(Children's Press, 2005)

Dividing Treasures
by Loren I. Charles
(Capstone Press, 2011)

Division Made Easy
by Rebecca Wingard-Nelson
and Tom LaBaff
(Enslow Elementary, 2005)

The Great Divide
by Danielle Carroll
(Yellow Umbrella Books, 2006)

If You Were a Divided-By Sign
by Trisha Speed Shaskan
and Sarah Dillard
(Picture Window Books, 2009)

Mathemagic! Number Tricks
by Lynda Colgan and others
(Kids Can Press, 2011)

WEBSITES

ABCYa! Division Drag Race
http://www.abcya.com/
division_drag_race.htm
The faster you can divide, the faster you
can drive in this practice game.

Division Games
http://www.divisiongames.net/
Arcade games at this site let you battle
invaders from space with your sharp
division skills!

Fun 4 the Brain: Division
http://www.fun4thebrain.com/division.html
Pick up essential division skills with the
games and printable worksheets at this
educational website.

Kids' Numbers: Division
http://www.kidsnumbers.com/division.php
Build strong division skills with lessons and
games that go week by week.

My Math Games: Division
http://www.learninggamesforkids.com/
math_division_games.html
Practice your division facts with flash
cards and games.

Play Kids' Games: Math Games
http://www.playkidsgames.com/
mathGames.htm
Test all of your math skills with this
site's wide variety of games.

NOTE TO EDUCATORS

This volume supports a conceptual understanding of division through a series of story problems. As Division and the other operations characters work to solve each story problem, they present different strategies, including variations of direct modeling, counting, and invented strategies. Below is an index of strategies that appear in this volume. For more information about how to use these strategies in the classroom, see the list of Educator Resources at the bottom of this page.

Index of Strategies

Educator Resources

Children's Mathematics: Cognitively Guided Instruction
  by Thomas Carpenter, Elizabeth Fennema, Megan L. Franke, Linda Levi, and Susan B. Empson (Heinemann, 1999)

Elementary and Middle School Mathematics: Teaching Developmentally
  by John A. Van de Walle, Karen S. Karp, and Jennifer M. Bay-Williams (Harcourt, 2013)

Knowing and Teaching Elementary Mathematics: Teachers' Understanding of Fundamental Mathematics in China and the United States
  by Liping Ma (Routledge, 2010)

Young Mathematicians at Work:
Constructing Multiplication and Division
  by Catherine Twomey Fosnot and Maarten Dolk (Heinemann, 2001)

Contents

Acknowledgments

It was with the best possible guidance and assistance that I undertook this project. My thanks to Lefty Kreh for sharing his formidable book-writing and book-proposing experience; to Nick Lyons for his solid advice (and patience with my many questions); to Brian Rose for his diligence and keen photographic eye; to Vic Erickson for giving this the full extent of his drafting and artistic talent; to Angela Babin of the Center for Safety in the Arts for her invaluable advice and the good work she is doing; to Dave Hughes for his constant support in my rod-building endeavors over the years; to Marty and Joyce Sherman—good friends who have always cared, professionally and personally; to Kerry Burkheimer for the countless hours we've shared absorbed in the mysteries of fly-rod design; to Paul and Lois Morris, who have always believed in their son—no matter how unconventional his pursuits and goals. And most of all to Russ Peak.

Foreword

When you fish constantly on one kind of water, you wish for a rod that is exactly right for that kind of fishing. I grew up fishing tiny plunge-pool streams in the coastal hills of Oregon, coaxing their native cutthroat trout up to take dry flies. Years later, in a chapter of *An Angler's Astoria*, I wrote about the rods I had used, and speculated about the rod that would be perfect. The rod I wished for would be a seven-footer for a #4 line; it would be light and bossy and quick.

Skip Morris read the book. I got a letter from him. "I'd like to build that rod you wrote about," he told me.

I agreed reluctantly. A wish is one thing, but I knew how hard it would be to build a fly rod from a description in a book. But Skip went at it. He started by duplicating in graphite the action of a small and graceful Granger bamboo owned by Rick Hafele, co-author of *Western Hatches*. Then Skip tuned the blank to my casting stroke. While in this stage it was an alarming looking thing, with the handle and guides taped to the blank for each casting session. Skip ran around me while I cast, asking questions and writing in a notebook. Then back to work he went. Each time I cast it the rod got a bit better.

When I received the finished rod, weeks later, I was amazed at its subtle beauty. I'd been looking at the try rod too long. When I took the rod astream, I was astonished at its performance. It did all the things I had always wanted a small-stream rod to do. It did them better than I was aware they could be done. I was suddenly a better caster than I thought I was.

When somebody delivers more than you expect, it's always a pleasant surprise. Skip did that when he delivered his rod to me. Skip knows fly rods, fly-rod design, fly-rod building. Now he's written a book about it, and again he has delivered more than expected.

The Custom Graphite Fly Rod will walk you through the

steps in building a fly rod from a blank, which is a relief, because a lot of books on rod building lead you out on limbs and leave you stranded there. Not this one. You start with an empty bench and a rod blank. Careful chapters tell you how to install all the various kinds of reelseats, construct and shape cork grips, wrap the guides, and finish the rod. When you're finished, Skip tells you how to put an inscription on it. His instructions are clear and detailed; if you follow them with the patience that he advises, you will own a rod you are proud to sign.

An early chapter tells you how to select a shaft that does what you want the rod to do. There are some surprises here. In the first place, Skip relates blank selection to fishing, which is unusual. Most rod-building folks relate it to casting, which is part of fishing but not all of it. Then he clarifies the *fast action* vs. *slow action* argument by recommending sensibly that we talk instead about rods that are *stiff-butted* or *soft-butted*. This chapter makes sense of things that have been puzzles to me for a long time.

Skip has only got you started when he's got you finished building a fly rod. He also tells you how to repair rods, and from there marches on to untrod ground by telling you how to strip the finish from a factory blank and alter its action to suit yourself. Before you are finished with the book you will be reading in the world of rod design. If you want, you can work in it, too.

The value of these chapters extends to those who have no intention to tinker with rod actions: it is a look into how rods are designed and how the designs are executed in glass and graphite. It is information that will help you select your first blank, your next blank, or even a completed fly rod.

Many people believe that the only reason to build a rod is to save money. That's a good reason, but it's not the only one. Building your own rod will help you wind up with precisely the right rod when you go fishing, no matter what kind of fly fishing you do. And, if you care to take the time, crafting your own rod will put you on the water with one that is classier than one you can buy.

Now, if you will excuse me, I'm going to slip down to the basement while you read on and Skip shows you how to build a rod. Reading this book has got me enthused; I've got to go fiddle with a blank I just bought.

DAVE HUGHES
Astoria, Oregon

THE CUSTOM
GRAPHITE FLY ROD

1 *Selecting Components*

The heart of a fly rod is its rod shafts, known together as a rod blank or simply a blank. For many years fly-rod blanks were constructed of various woods, but in 1946 both the Shakespeare and Conolon Companies introduced the first fiberglass rods, setting a precedent that would change the concept of fly-rod design forever. But the glass fly rod was only in its first stages of development; its potential was barely tapped. Fiberglass fly rods were soon characterized as inexpensive, inferior substitutes for fly rods of bamboo. Rod maker/rod designer Russ Peak pioneered the idea of high-performance glass fly rods and from his brilliant research and exquisite craftsmanship created rods that gave this idea credence.

In 1974 the Fenwick Rod Company unveiled the first graphite fly rods; graphite suddenly became the most talked about fly-rod material. As designs and technology have improved over the years, graphite has become the most popular fly-rod material by a landslide.

The Rod Blank

Blank selection is critical as this will determine the performance of your finished rod. In discussing the performance characteristics of rod shafts, it is important to differentiate between rod action and rod response. First, rod action. My definition is as follows: rod action describes the curve created in a rod during casting. My definition of rod response is this: rod response describes the degree of quickness with which a rod transfers the caster's movements to the line. Let's begin by exploring fly-rod action.

Though there are many times when a fly rod is flexed in a day's fishing, I feel that, with regard to action, the curve created in a rod during casting is the most telling. This is simply because the rod is in motion and kinetic energy (mass in motion) will exert its normal influence on the relationship between tip flex and butt flex. In other words, tip weight will be greatly magnified during casting and force the butt to flex more markedly than some static test. A deflection board, for example, consists of a grid and a rod, secured by its grip, with a weight suspended from its point. The curve of the rod can be plotted against the grid, but, as the rod is static, tip weight will have only a minor effect on butt flex; increase the weight of that tip only a few fractions of an ounce and it probably won't show up on a deflection board, but cast that same rod and the difference in flex and performance may be dramatic.

In general, I divide rod action into the three categories of fast (stiff-butted), slow (soft-butted), and moderate. Here are my definitions.

Fast action: a rod in which the butt flexes very little while the relatively supple tip performs almost all the chores of loading and flexing. An extremely fast-action rod may flex almost entirely in the upper part of the tip section. I think the term "stiff-butted" is clearer than the term "fast action."

Slow action: a rod in which the butt flexes quite actively and can be felt working even on fairly short casts. The tip section is usually quite stiff; this drives the flexing down into the butt. However, if the butt is supple enough, a slow-action rod will result even with a relatively supple tip section. Here again, another term, soft-butted, may provide a clearer image.

Moderate action: an action between fast and slow. Neither especially stiff nor supple in the butt section.

The other main category for describing fly-rod performance

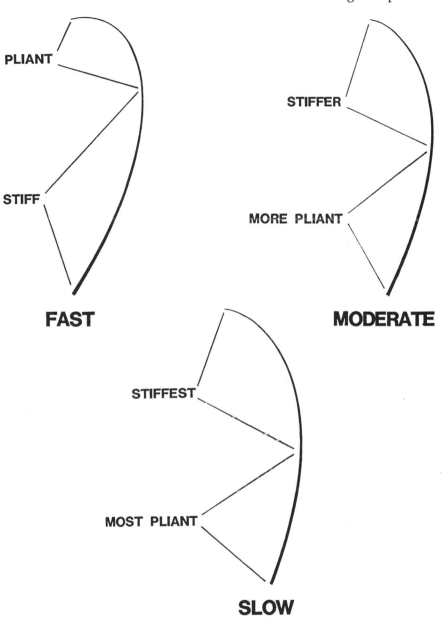

FAST

MODERATE

SLOW

ROD ACTION

is rod response, or "feel," which describes a rod's quickness to respond. I believe that the confusion often associated with rod action and response exists because these characteristics usually parallel each other. Fast-action rods generally have a fast response and slow-action rods a slow response. But the exceptions are many. Take, for example, a rod possessing a lightweight tip and plenty of power overall. Although the rod action is slow, the response will be quick. The angler describing both these qualities with a single word, like "fast," is half right and half wrong.

For the most part a rod somewhere in the broad range of moderate action will please almost any angler and will prove the most versatile. Experienced fly fishermen, however, often develop specific tastes regarding rod action and unless angling conditions strongly dictate otherwise, these anglers should follow their tastes.

It is important to understand how rod action relates to the functions of angling; the following information will provide a useful guide. Slow-action rods can be fine with all lines and flies but have a special advantage with sinking lines or weighted flies or both. Small-diameter sinking lines must travel at higher speeds than floating lines to stay airborn; this, combined with a low wind resistance, can cause a tight loop to turn over with a clumsy jerk. Weighted flies will do the same. What is needed is a wider loop and more gradual acceleration during a casting stroke; this is achieved by the slower rod's softer butt section. For many anglers softer-butted rods aid in delivering a fly with minimal disturbance on the water—a critical factor when faced with clear water and trout that are wary. Slower rods also load especially well on short casts, as the tip's length, mass, and stiffness tend to force the supple butt to flex on even a short length of line.

Fast-action rods tend to throw tight loops, which is useful for distance casting, casting in wind, and drawing the moisture from a dry fly. Stiff-butted rods also help the angler drive a hook into large or hard-mouthed fish and aid in controling really big fish.

Moderate-action rods do it all well. While one might sometimes wish for a slower rod to handle a sinking line or a bit faster rod when distance is needed, the moderate-action rod is a safe compromise; its versatility insures that it will most often perform honorably.

Also important is rod length. In my experience, shorter rods lend themselves to fast-to-moderate actions while longer rods lend themselves to moderate-to-slow actions. But exceptions to this rule are many.

Rod length involves other considerations having little to do with action. Short rods, say 7 1/2' or less, are especially kind to fragile leaders; they are also a good choice for short casts or small streams or both. Long rods, over nine feet, offer increased line control and higher backcasts, although I feel that they do not necessarily increase casting range as many anglers assume. Middle-length rods, around eight to nine feet, are usually my first choice and while nine feet has become almost the standard for practically any kind of fishing, I feel that a rod of around 8 1/2' is usually the most versatile and practical.

A fly-rod blank is designed to cast one or more sizes of fly lines. A rod's action and length have little to do with the line or lines it will properly cast: the deciding factor is power. The sizing system used for fly lines is based on the weight of the first thirty feet of line. Most fly lines run from a #2 (extremely light) to a #13 (extremely heavy). Generally #2 and #3 lines are reserved for special ultralight duty; the flies and conditions they handle best are quite limited. Lines #4 and #5 should still be considered light, but cover well the whole light-duty angling spectrum. Lines #6 and #7 are the middle weights and offer great versatility. Lines from #8 up (some might say from #7) are big lines for such big fish as really large trout, salmon, bass, and powerful saltwater species.

The subject of fly-line design is a different matter. Suffice to say that fly lines come in two basic styles—weight forward and double taper. Since the first thirty feet of all fly lines of the same size will weigh the same regardless of taper, a cast of about fifty feet or less (thirty feet of line plus leader plus length of horizontal rod) will be virtually identical with either line style. If you intend to be casting long most of the time, which most anglers don't, consider using a line one size heavier if you select a weight-forward line over a double taper.

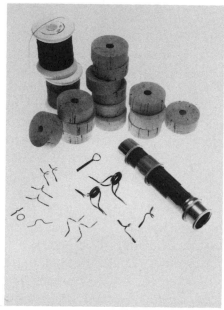

Components for rodmaking.

The Reel Seat

While rod-blank selection is your most important decision with regards to function, also important is your choice of reel seat. Reel seats, along with the various other parts of a fly rod, are often called components; the blank is generally not referred to as a component.

On light-line rods you may use a cork filler and one or two sliding lock rings for a reel seat. A variation of this is the wood-filler sliding lock-ring reel seat. Another possibility, which may be slightly more secure in its hold on the reel, is the wood-filler screw-lock seat. A simple all-metal reel seat can be the least expensive, although there are some of fine quality. I prefer to use the wood-filler or all-metal seat on rods casting lines #6 or heavier. A heavily anodized all-aluminum seat will best resist corrosion on a saltwater rod.

Almost all reel seats today are offered in either uplocking style, which tightens toward the tip, or downlocking style,

Left to right: downlocking cork-and-slide-band seat, uplocking cork-and-slide-band seat, cork-and-two-slide-band seat, uplocking wood-filler screw-lock seat, downlocking wood-filler screw-lock seat, all-metal reel seat.

which tightens toward the blank's base. There has been a lot of discussion about which is best; in my experience, they are both comparable functionally.

The wood-filler and all-metal seats generally come complete, requiring only assembly; to make the different cork-filler seats you will need to collect a few items. The downlocking seat will require eight cork rings, a sliding band, and a hooded butt cap. The uplocking style will require eight cork rings, a sliding band, an open hood, and a butt plate. A double-band seat will require eight cork rings, two slide bands, and a butt plate.

The Grip

On almost all my rods I use fourteen 1/2" cork rings to form a 7" grip. This has proven large enough for almost anyone's hand, although a few anglers might prefer fifteen or sixteen corks for a rod that is really heavy duty. Get the best-quality corks you can find—those with the fewest holes, referred to as pits. If possible, hand select your cork. I get almost all my cork with 1/4" holes but if you can get cork that has a hole only slightly smaller than the diameter of the blank where the grip will be formed it will later save you some filing. You won't need any cork rings for the grip if you use a preformed grip—unless you want to combine it with an uplocking reel seat and a recessed hood; in this case purchase two cork rings along with your preformed grip. I like to wrap thread over the front of a grip that is formed on the blank. With preformed grips and grips formed off the blank you will need a winding check—a metal, plastic, or rubber ring that seats up against the front of the grip for a neat appearance. Chapter 3 discusses grip styles, grip construction, and winding checks.

If you plan to put a removable or permanent fighting butt on your rod—as some prefer for heavy-duty rods—you will need four additional corks.

Lower left is a badly pitted cork; the cork on the upper right is much denser, much better.

Guides

I always use chrome-plated snake guides for intermediates. These guides are light, tough, adequately flexible, and, because of the hard chrome plating, offer excellent resistance to wear.

The classic chrome-plated pear-shaped tip top is usually my first choice. For a stripper guide a good choice is one with a tough wear-resistant inner ring made of aluminum oxide or silicone carbide. Some anglers prefer two stripper guides on rods nine feet or longer although this is mostly for appearance. Chapter 4 has charts to help you select the right size and number of guides.

Hook-keepers are standard but optional. Most common are the simple stainless-steel hump or the loose ring; select whichever appeals to you.

You will need at least one hundred-yard spool of nylon size A rod-winding thread for the main wraps and, if you like, one or more additional spools for trim. Chapter 4 discusses thread colors and aesthetics.

As you proceed, you will find that there are a few tools and items you will need in addition to what we have covered here: I have kept their cost and number to a minimum.

Now it is time to begin construction of your new rod.

2 *Reel Seats*

With your components selected, your first construction step will be to mount your reel seat onto the butt section of your blank. To do this properly you must start by finding the butt's spine. The term "spine" refers to a blank's stiff side. It is best for the guides and reel to be opposite the spine—on the blank's soft side; during a cast, this will help keep the rod aligned.

Finding the Spine

To determine the spine, place the base of the butt section on a flat, smooth, hard, horizontal surface and rest the butt's point in your hand a foot or two above that surface. With your other hand press down on the center of the butt and roll the section slowly. Most rod sections will reveal a spine—some sections will almost jump in your hand as the stiff spine takes command; others will have a slight spine that it is almost undetectable. Directly opposite the spine, on the underside of the blank, is the side you want to be in line with the guides and reel. Wrap a piece of masking tape around the center of the butt section and with a pen mark this opposite side of the spine—the soft side.

Spining the butt section.

Wood-Filler Reel Seats

We will start with wood-filler screw-lock seats since they are popular. Begin by assembling the seat and test fitting it to the reel you plan to use on the rod. If all fits, fine; if not, you may have to shorten the wood filler to fit. Saw off only a small amount at a time and keep the filler as long as possible to insure that other reels will fit should you ever make a change.

The reel seat will be mounted on the very base of the butt section. To test fit, push the point of the butt into the hole in the center of the wood filler. Slide the filler toward the base of the butt section as far as it will go. If the filler slides over the base of the butt and off, you will need to shim. If the reel seat stops tight somewhere up the butt, you will either have to ream the filler or use another seat. If you lead a charmed life, your reel seat will tighten in place just as it reaches the base of your butt section; but since most mortals, me included, rarely experience this kind of dumb luck, I will explain shimming and reaming.

Before shimming, thoroughly sand the area that will hold

the reel seat with #220 sandpaper; this will provide tooth for a good glue bond later. Next, take a strip of 3/4″ masking tape and cut it in half lengthwise. Take one of the resulting 3/8″ strips and wrap it around the base of the butt section. After a few turns, tear off the end of the tape and check to see if the wood filler now fits. Continue wrapping and check fitting until the filler fits in place snugly. Next wrap some 3/8″ masking tape around the area where the upper end of the wood filler will be mounted until you have a good fit here too.

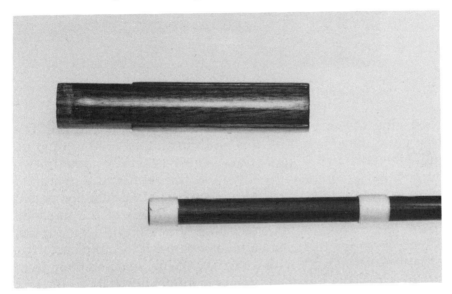

Shimming the butt to fit a wood filler.

To ream out a filler, use a drill press, or a hand drill, and an appropriate-sized woodboring bit. Work slowly and remove only a little at a time to avoid splitting the filler. If the blank is so large that you will have to thin the walls of the wood filler to less than 1/8″ thick, then don't ream. Instead, substitute an all-metal seat that will have a larger opening. You can also ream your filler with a rattail file.

Preassembling your wood-filler reel seat is the safest, neatest approach. Start by using a strip of #100 sandpaper wrapped over a piece of scrap blank to rough up the inside surface of both your threaded barrel and metal cap thoroughly. Be especially thorough if your metal parts are made of nickel silver.

A strip of sandpaper looped over a section of scrap blank.

Next glue the screw-lock parts onto the threaded barrel. The best glue I have found for this and most other rod-building requirements is a slow-cure epoxy. These generally come in two components, require a fifty-fifty mix, and set up fully in around eight to twenty-four hours. Mix a batch of slow-cure epoxy and spread a thin layer on both the inside surface of the threaded barrel and the part of the wood filler where it will be mounted. Slowly twist the threaded barrel as you push it into place; wipe off any excess epoxy with a rag; also, wipe excess epoxy from the inside of the threaded barrel on uplocking seats so the end plug will fit later. Set the filler on its end, threaded barrel up, to cure overnight.

You will have a little extra work to perform if the reel seat you have selected is uplocking. The cap on uplocking reel seats may be a perfect circle or it may be hooded. In either case you will want to bury the hood in a cork ring. Press the face of your hood into the flat side of an especially fine cork ring. When you remove the hood, it will have left an impression. Using a rattail file, work the hole in the cork ring out to the shape of this impression. Your hood should now fit snugly into your cork ring. With #100 sandpaper, thoroughly sand the outside surface of your reel-seat cap. Smear some slow-cure epoxy inside the cork and a little on the reel seat cap. Push the rear of the cap into the cork until the cork extends about 1/16″ beyond the front of the

Stages for preparing a hood cork.

cap. With a rag wipe off any excess epoxy that has squeezed out. Next, to obtain a really tight impressive fit between cap and cork, wrap the front edge of the cork with ten to fifteen tight turns of heavy thread, like size E rod-winding thread. Again wipe off any excess epoxy that has squeezed out. Tie off the thread and set all aside to cure overnight. The next day you can lay the face of the cork flat on a sheet of sandpaper; then, by working the cork back and forth, remove the epoxy stains and work the cork back to a point just short of the cap. Start with #220 sandpaper followed by #320 and finishing with #400. The result should be a cork and cap exemplifying fine crafts-manship.

Before mounting an uplocking wood-filler reel seat on the butt, you will want to mount the cap in place. Use slow-cure epoxy and smear it only in the cap, not on the wood filler. You will not want to mount the cap on a downlocking seat until the rod is essentially completed.

Mount either the uplock or downlock wood-filler seat on the base of the butt section simply by sliding it down into place over a layer of slow-cure epoxy. Twist the reel seat as you slowly push it into place. If the epoxy builds up too heavily, back the seat off and wipe some away. Again, wipe out any epoxy that might block the end plug from later mounting inside the barrel of an uplocking reel seat. Be certain, also, that no epoxy is left inside the base of the butt; you can wipe it out with strips of fabric looped over a stick or piece of scrap blank.

Wood-filler Slide-Band Reel Seats

The process for mounting the wood-filler slide-band reel seat is essentially the same one used for mounting the wood-filler screw-lock reel seat, the only difference being that there is less hardware to mount. Usually the wood-filler slide-band seat consists of a wood filler, a slide band, a butt cap, and a cork check.

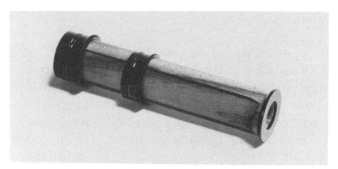

A wood-filler slide-band reel seat.

The slide band and butt cap should not be mounted until the rod is completed. The cork check—a metal ring that mounts on the upper end of the wood filler, up against the rear of the cork grip—can be mounted with a tiny amount of slow-cure epoxy, just before mounting the grip. The cork check is held in place more by the pressure fit between reel seat and grip than by the epoxy.

All-Metal Reel Seats and the Turning System

The all-metal reel seat has a large enough opening to accommodate almost any blank. If the fit is close, you can shim with strips of masking tape as previously outlined for the wood-filler seat. If not, you will need a larger shim made from cork rings. To accomplish this you will need a turning system. The idea is to get your work spinning rapidly enough that you can shape the cork with sandpaper. An electric drill secured in a drill stand will work as will a bench grinder mounted on one end

with a drill chuck. Twenty to thirty thousand R.P.M.s will be required. Be sure to refer to Chapter 9 on shop safety before using your turning system.

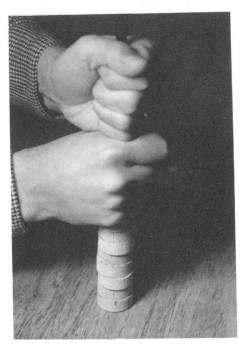

Compressing corks for a metal reel-seat shim.

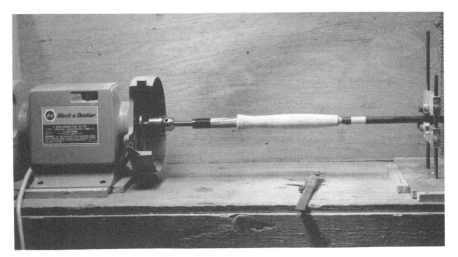

A turning system.

Mount the cork rings on the butt section, where the seat will be mounted, with slow-cure epoxy. Push about a 6″ section of scrap blank shimmed with two bands of 3/4″ masking tape into the base of your butt section and chuck the scrap section in your turning system. You will need to steady the other end of your butt section as it is turning. You can purchase premade

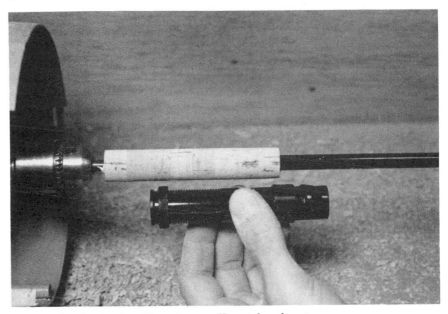

Cork cylinder for shimming an all-metal reel seat.

supports from some of the rod-building supply houses or make your own using a bit of ingenuity. I always protect the blank, where it mounts in a support, with a piece of scrap blank shimmed with masking tape. This way if, for some reason, the support causes a gouge, it will be in the scrap blank, not the good one. Start your turning system and turn the cork down to a cylinder equal to the inside of your reel seat in diameter. Two supports, one near the base and the other near the point of the butt, will leave both hands free. Only one support, near the butt's base, will require you to steady the section with one hand. After dressing the cork cylinder to size, remove the work from your turning system and spread a thin layer of slow-cure epoxy onto the cork and the inside of the reel seat. Twist the reel seat as you slowly push it up in place. Wipe off any excess epoxy and

set all aside to cure overnight.

If you decide to mount your all-metal reel seat so it is up-locking, you may want to bury the cap in a cork. Since you won't be able to make an impression in the cork because the cap is premounted, simply enlarge the hole in the cork with a rattail file until it fits the cap. Put slow-cure epoxy inside the cork *only* and slide the cork over the cap from the end of the reel seat. Compress the cork with turns of thread as described earlier and carefully remove any epoxy that squeezes out. Try not to let the epoxy stain the face of the cork as you will not be able to dress the cork later.

The Removable Fighting Butt

For big fish rods you may want to combine an all-metal or wood-filler reel seat with a removable fighting butt. For this, your butt section must be reinforced. Sand, with #220 sand-paper, the last 1/2" at the base of your butt section down to bare graphite. Remove a long strand from a sheet of woven fiberglass (available in hardware stores). At the very rim of your butt section's base wrap the fiberglass strand over itself to lock it in place. Spiral the glass strand, in close turns, up the 1/2" of bare material; use only moderate pressure as glass in this state is fragile. Next make a few wide spirals of the strand and lock it in place with a piece of masking tape. About 10" from a heat lamp

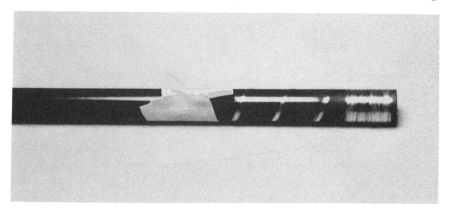

Base of butt section wrapped with glass strand for removable fighting butt.

Adding epoxy to a glass reinforcement for a fighting butt; note the heat lamp in the upper right corner.

saturate the close turns of glass with slow-cure epoxy—the heat will make the epoxy thin and flow. Set your butt section in a horizontal position to cure; give it a quarter turn occasionally to keep the epoxy from sagging and don't let the epoxy touch anything unless you want the bench or box under your blank to become a permanent part of your finished rod. Another way to keep the uncured epoxy from sagging is to mount the butt section in a rotation system as described in Chapter 4 for curing finish.

When the epoxy has cured, remove the masking tape and cut off the glass strand where it is not epoxied. Next, push a section of sturdy scrap blank, small end first, into the base of your butt section until it fits snugly. Mark the point at the bottom rim of the butt section on the scrap blank. Remove the scrap blank and cut it off 3″ above the mark toward its small end using a grinding wheel. Replace the scrap blank in your butt section and note if it again stops at the mark you made before. If it does, set aside the scrap blank and epoxy your reel seat in place; make sure the butt is far enough up the reel seat to leave room for a removable plug or button if you plan to use one.

When the epoxy has cured, re-insert your scrap blank and mark it at 1 7/8″ from the edge of your reel seat. Cut the scrap blank at this mark. Next, with a rattail file enlarge the openings in two cork rings to slide easily over the rear portion of the scrap blank. Enlarge the openings in two more corks to fit over the scrap blank tightly. Smear some slow-cure epoxy onto the rear of the scrap blank and slide a tight-fitting cork down until it extends slightly over the rim of your scrap blank's base. With a Popsicle stick or similar object, smear a thin layer of the epoxy on the face of the cork you just mounted, so that the next cork will contact the epoxy. Add a little more epoxy just ahead of the first cork and slide a loose-fitting cork down your scrap blank. Spin the second cork slowly as you push it up against the first. Add another loose-fitting cork, and then the other tight-fitting cork in this fashion. Do not smear epoxy on the outside face of the last cork. Press the corks together tight, then set your fighting butt aside to cure overnight.

The next day, wrap a few turns of masking tape around the bare shaft of your fighting butt and chuck it up in your turning system. Dress the corks to a 1″ cylinder rounded at the rear edge; you can also taper the front of the corks to match the reel seat's diameter. Be sure to dress the face of the end cork to remove any epoxy stains.

A Dremel tool with a fluted bit will quickly rough-shape your fighting butt. Simply work the bit, on full speed, up and down the cork, taking care not to let the bit gouge in. Follow with strips of sandpaper worked across the spinning fighting butt similar to performing a shoe shine. Start with #100 sandpaper followed by #220 and ending with #320. Final finishing and filling the natural holes in the cork (called pits) will be required later and is covered in Chapter 3.

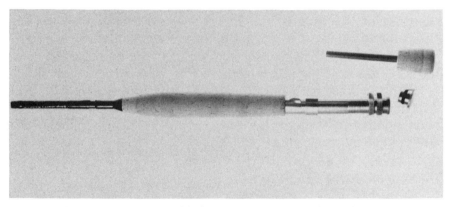

Finished rod with removable butt plug and removable fighting butt.

Cork-and-Slide-Band Reel Seats

As described in Chapter 1, there are three basic styles of cork-and-slide-band reel seat: downlocking with a cap, uplocking with a cap, and the two-slide-band style with a butt plate. We will begin with the downlocking style.

With a rattail file enlarge the holes in eight cork rings to fit over the base of your butt section; six of the corks should slide on easily, but two should fit tightly. As always, rough up the blank's finish where the reel seat will be formed with #100 sandpaper. Next, smear some slow-cure epoxy on the base of the butt section and slide one of the tight-fitting corks in place—flush with the lower rim of the butt section. Wipe off any excess epoxy—especially any that might get inside the butt section. With a flat Popsicle stick or similar object smear a thin, even layer of epoxy on the face of the tight-fitting cork where the next cork will contact it. Smear a little more epoxy on the butt and slide a loose-fitting cork down the butt section. Continue this sequence, ending with the other tight-fitting cork. Place your butt section, base down, on a hard flat surface and push down on the top cork. The tight-fitting corks on the ends will hold this compression and produce thin neat glue lines. Set all aside to cure overnight.

After the epoxy has cured, push a short piece of scrap blank snugly into the base of your butt section and use a masking-tape shim to hold another section of scrap blank in place where the rod support makes contact—as previously described for making a cork shim for an all-metal reel seat.

Dress the corks down to a cylinder slightly larger than your cap or slide band; then, using #320 sandpaper, turn the cylinder down to the point where the cap just fits in place.

If your end cap has a hood, all you need do is dress the remainder of the corks until the slide band fits comfortably over the foot of the reel you have chosen. If, however, you have an end cap that forms a perfect circle, you will need to sand a flattened area on the cork cylinder.

To sand a flattened area, start with #100 sandpaper and make long strokes down the cylinder's full length. The flattened area should form a mild curve in cross section. When the reel almost fits the cap and band, start working through #220, then #320 sandpaper to get a good fit.

The procedures we just covered, with a few exceptions, are the same as those used to make the uplocking cap-and-ring seat. Glue up the cork rings as you did for the downlock cap-and-ring reel seat and, after the epoxy has cured, chuck your butt section up into your turning system. Dress the corks to cylindrical shape, but form a flared or bell-shaped end in the cork at the base of the butt section. Mount a cork on the cap, as described previously for the uplocking wood-filler reel seat, and work through #220 and #320 until your reel fits properly in place. Here again, you will have to form a flattened area on the cylinder if your cap forms a perfect circle. Do not epoxy the cap in place until you have filled the natural holes (called pits) in the cork and have given the cylinder its final sanding with #400 sandpaper—both of which will be covered in Chapter 3.

The double-slide-band reel seat is shaped just like the up-lock-slide-band seat (flared at the base) but without any cap. The reel mounts between the bands with one band pushed onto each end of the reel's tang. You can fit the reel by forming a flattened area on the cylinder or by dressing the cylinder to a small enough diameter to leave adequate space between cork and slide band. The front lips on the slide bands should be facing one another.

3 Cork Grips

Although many fly rods on today's market have grips of only 6″ or 6 1/2″, I have always preferred a 7″ grip. For a big-fish rod I may make a grip longer than 7″, but rarely will I make one shorter. A 7″ grip will, predictably, require fourteen 1/2″ cork rings.

The four grip styles I have used most often are very popular: the full Wells, half Wells, reversed half Wells, and torpedo. The Wells series of grips were named for nineteenth-century fly-fishing writer Henry Wells.

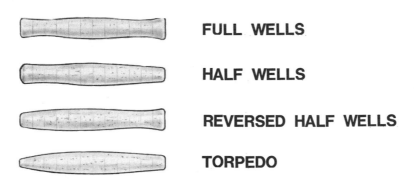

FULL WELLS

HALF WELLS

REVERSED HALF WELLS

TORPEDO

GRIP STYLES

The full Wells has a flare at each end and a swell in the center. Removing the flare from the rear of a full Wells grip will result in a half Wells; removing the flare from the front of a full Wells grip will result in a reversed half Wells. The torpedo grip has no flares, simply a swell in the center with a gradual front taper. Similar to the torpedo grip is the cigar grip with a swell in the center, no flares, and blunt ends. All of these grips are attractive and functional and can be used on any rod. Whichever grip you choose, keep the curves gradual and flowing to insure casting comfort.

The simplest answer for a grip is to purchase a preformed one. Simply ream the inside of the grip to size with a rattail file and mount. If you want to use an uplocking reel seat and recess it into your grip, start by sliding the premade grip onto a scrap blank section and mounting both in your turning system. Using your Dremel tool and a fluted bit, cut off the last two corks. Smooth the rear of the grip to a flat plane with #100 sandpaper. Mount the reel-seat hood in a cork ring and mount the hood on the reel seat as described in Chapter 2. The next day, mount the preformed grip up against the reel-seat hood cork (two corks may be required for a long hood; mount the second cork just before adding the grip). After gluing, press the grip firmly into place; if the opening in the grip fits snugly, you will have a good compression. If not, a few rubber bands stretched the length of the grip will compress it. Let the glue set up. To complete, dress the cork ring (rings) in your turning system until they flow into the shape of your grip.

Another approach is to form your grip from cork rings glued up on a length of 1/4″ threaded rod. Smear slow-cure epoxy on the face of each cork before sliding the next up against it. Leave the last 1/8″ of each cork, near the threaded rod, clear of epoxy; this way the grip will slip easily off later. A nut at each end of the glued-up cork will allow you to tighten everything up for good compression. The next day you can mount the corks, still on the threaded rod, into your turning system and shape the grip.

If your reel seat is uplocking and you want the hood recessed into the rear of your grip, prepare the last cork, or corks, to fit the reel-seat hood as described in Chapter 2. Glue the hood cork, or corks, last; check for centering and slide on a last

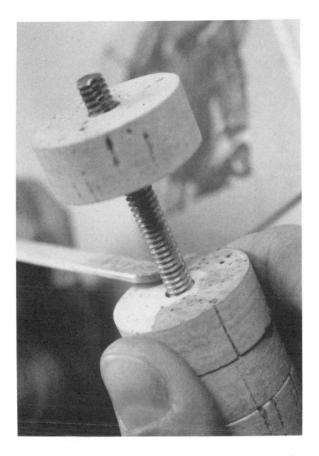

Gluing corks on a threaded rod; note that the epoxy stops clear of the threaded rod.

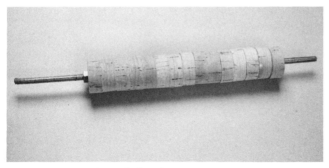

Corks glued up on a threaded rod.

cork with no epoxy. Tighten everything up. The next day, re-move the end cork, tighten the nut up inside the hood cork, or corks, and shape as usual. Fill the pits and dress the filler as described in this chapter. Smear some slow-cure epoxy inside the hood cork just before gluing the grip in place.

When reaming out preformed grips or grips turned off the rod, try to keep the hole centered and even. File a shallow bevel around the rear opening of the grip to catch excess glue. Sand the blank where the grip will mount. Smear a layer of glue over this sanded area and twist/push the grip slowly into place. If the glue builds up too thick against the rear of the grip, stop, back the grip off a little, and wipe off the excess with a rag. A glue called Urethane bond is good for off-the-blank grips be-cause it swells as it dries, filling any open spaces.

Forming the bevel that aids in gluing on a preformed grip.

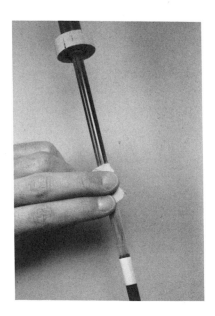

Sanding the blank where the grip will be mounted.

Any preformed or built-off-the-blank grip will probably, for best appearance, require a winding check. Winding checks are available in metal, plastic, or rubber; the flexible rubber checks are easiest to fit. The only drawback with rubber checks, primarily the really soft ones, is that they may deteriorate with age. Measure the outside diameter of your blank at the winding-check location at the front of the grip and order the best-fitting check or take your blank to a fly shop where you can test-fit winding checks directly on your blank. A little slow-cure epoxy will hold the check in place until the thread wraps and finish really secure it.

The most secure grip is one formed on the blank; this grip construction also allows you to taper the front of the grip to the blank and blend the connection with thread wraps—an elegant look.

If your reel seat is uplocking, you will only need thirteen cork rings as your first cork is already mounted on the reel-seat cap. The caps on some uplocking seats are longer than 1/2" and will extend beyond the cork; this requires that the next cork be reamed with a rattail file or Dremel tool until both corks fit flush.

Before gluing the corks in place you will want to arrange them in order. First, set aside four of the clearest corks (freest of pits) for the front of your grip. This is a critical area for stress as considerable pressure is exerted by the small area at the pad of the caster's thumb. Try to arrange the remaining corks so that the largest pits will either be dressed off when you shape the grip or hidden beneath its surface.

Since your reel seat will anchor the lower end of the grip, enlarge the holes in all your corks (except the front or "face" cork) to fit loosely. The face cork should fit tightly. An even fit, with no gaps, will be helpful later since you will be wrapping thread from the blank up onto the cork.

If you have a cork-and-slide-band reel seat, now is the time to fill the pits. First, use a toothpick to clean any loose material from the pits in your reel seat. Next, make a mixture of about 50 percent cork dust (left from dressing the reel seat), about 50 percent Weldwood Plastic Resin Glue, a few drops of white poster paint, and some water. Mix these into a paste using a plastic knife or plastic spoon; try to get the color of the mixture

Compressing a built-on-the-blank grip.

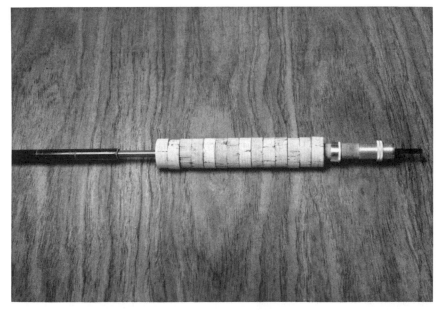

On-the-blank grip ready to chuck into a turning system.

close to the color of the cork. With the knife or spoon, press some of the paste into the pits and set all aside to dry overnight.

The next day, chuck your butt section up in your turning system, start everything spinning, and sand the cork reel seat with #320 sandpaper until all excess pit filler is dressed off. Finish with #400 sandpaper. If your cork filler has a flattened area, hand sand that area with #320 and #400 sandpaper. Now is the time to slip any slide bands onto the cork filler if your seat is uplocking or double-slide-band style. If your cork reel seat is uplocking style, rough up the inside of the cap with #100 sandpaper, smear some slow-cure epoxy around the inside of the hood where it will contact the cork (not where it will contact the reel foot) and push the cap in place. To avoid getting any epoxy on the blank during this process, apply the epoxy to the cap when it is only an inch or two in front of the reel seat; if you do get any epoxy on the blank, it will be cured under the grip. Set all aside to dry overnight.

Wood-filler screw-lock reel seats may require that some of the hardware is mounted before the grip is glued up; check this and attend to it if necessary. If your wood-filler reel seat is uplocking, epoxy the cap in place as just described for the uplocking cork and slide-band seat and set aside to cure overnight. Be

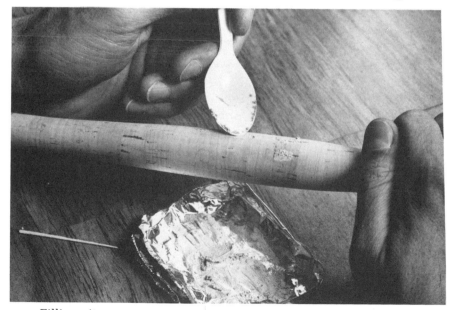

Filling pits.

certain the cork check is mounted before mounting your grip if you are using a wood-filler slide-band reel seat.

Glue up the corks for your grip as described in Chapter 2 for cork and slide-band reel seats. Set the base of your butt section (the reel seat) on a hard flat surface at a 90° angle and press down firmly on the face cork; this will compress the corks. Set all aside to cure overnight.

The next day, chuck your butt section up in your turning system as described in Chapter 2. Start the butt spinning; then, using your Dremel tool with a fluted bit or a strip of #80 sandpaper, dress the high spots on the cork so that you have an even, balanced cylinder. Continue rough dressing the grip until

Fluted Dremel bit.

Rough dressing with a Dremel tool and fluted bit.

you have its basic shape, oversize. Using strips of sandpaper, work through #100 and #220, ending with #320. I have found that the maximum diameter of a grip's center swell should be about 1″ to 1 1/16″ to please most anglers. For unusual tastes, or an especially heavy- or light-duty rod, you may want to vary those dimensions somewhat. A thicker grip may be more comfortable for a really big rod while a slender grip on a delicate light-line rod may offer sensitivity.

Trimming the grip's front to the blank with a single-edged razor blade.

You will want to taper the front of your grip down to the blank. Stop when the cork is about 1/16″ from the blank's surface. For the reversed half Wells and torpedo styles, taper the front of the grip down at a gradual angle. For the full Wells and half Wells leave a short lip in front. Sandpaper wrapped around a piece of scrap blank can be helpful in creating this lip. Your next job will be to taper the front edge of your face cork carefully down to the blank with a single-edged razor blade or a matt knife.

Filling the pits will complete your grip; proceed as described earlier in this chapter for cork and slide-band reel seats.

4 *Thread Wraps*

Thread Colors

With your reel seat and grip in place, it is time to add both decorative and functional thread wraps. The color of thread you choose will depend partly on your blank color. Rod companies seem to have settled on dark, subtle colors for fly-rod blanks: orange browns, reddish browns, black, and the natural dark gray of graphite, for example. I approach rod colors the same way I approach clothing colors—I would not wear a bright-blue shirt with orange pants and a lime-green tie, nor would I combine these colors in a fly rod. My preference is for subtle-but-complimentary thread colors. On a reddish brown blank I might use dark brown, dark red, or black thread. I might add a lighter thread color, sparingly, to brighten the rod, something like white, orange, or even yellow—but I'd have to see it first. Purchase several colors of thread if they catch your eye; rod-winding thread is inexpensive and an important part of your rod's appearance; later you can pick out the colors you prefer.

Test thread colors by wrapping samples on your blank. Then saturate the thread with water; this will be close to the thread's appearance when saturated with finish.

Some rodmakers keep thread colors bright by applying a product called color preserver. It is applied to thread wraps and allowed to dry before finish is applied. As color preserver dries, the original bright color returns to the thread. Finish can only form a sheath around the treated wraps as it cannot penetrate the coating of color preserver. I feel that a stronger bond is formed if finish saturates the thread wraps so I avoid using color preserver. Besides, I prefer the deep, translucent appearance thread wraps take on when finish is applied to them directly.

For short, bright thread wrappings, I often use N.C.P. thread. The N.C.P. stands for no color preserver, which means this thread keeps its color when finish is applied to it directly. N.C.P. thread looks sharp in small amounts but in a long wrap it tends to look dull. Regular rod-winding thread in light colors can also add highlights, even without color preserver.

Dressing Guides and Hookkeeper

Before wrapping on your guides and hookkeeper, you will need to dress them. The feet on guides and keepers are usually squared-off or, at best, tapered inadequately. Dress the tops of the feet against a grinding wheel or sharpening stone until they

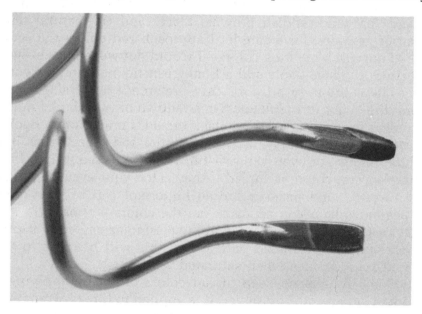

Properly ground guide foot on top; unground guide foot on bottom.

taper gradually to a rounded point. To remove any burrs that might damage your blank, gently dress the underside of your guides and hookkeeper against a sharpening stone. Rub your finger against the undersides of the feet to insure that all burrs are removed.

Dressing the underside of the guide feet on a sharpening stone.

Guide Spacing

Before wrapping your guides and keeper in place you must determine your guide spacing; the following chart will provide some useful guidelines.

As you may notice, I prefer that stripping guides be slightly closer to a rod's base on light-line and short fly rods than on heavier rods. The guides for the #8-line rod are the largest you will normally need, but on some saltwater rods I have gone up to size 5 and 6 snakes on the tip with a large-diameter spin-rod tip top. The spacings shown will work well for most rods, but for really soft-butted slow-action rods, it is wise to spread out the tip guides and close up the butt guides slightly; do the opposite on fast-action rods.

Guide Spacing Chart

Lines	Guides	Inches From Point Of Tip
7' #3 line	#1/0	5"
	#1/0	10 1/8"
	#1	15 1/4"
	#1	21"
	#1	27"
	#1	33 1/4"
	#2	40 1/4"
	#3	47 3/4"
	#8 stripping guide	56"
7' 6" #4 line	#1/0	5"
	#1	10 1/4"
	#1	15 7/8"
	#1	21 7/8"
	#1	28 3/8"
	#2	35 1/4"
	#2	43"
	#3	51 3/4"
	#8 stripping guide	61"
8' #5 line	#1	5"
	#1	10 1/4"
	#1	15 1/2"
	#1	21 3/8"
	#1	27 3/8"
	#2	33 3/4"
	#2	40 1/2"
	#3	47 7/8"
	#4	56 1/2"
	#10 stripping guide	66"
8' 6" #4 line	#1/0	5"
	#1	10 1/4"
	#1	15 7/8"
	#1	21 3/4"
	#1	28"
	#2	34 3/4"
	#2	41 3/4"
	#2	49 5/8"
	#3	59 3/4"
	#10 stripping guide	71 1/2"

Guide Spacing Chart

Lines	Guides	Inches From Point Of Tip
8' 6" #7 line	#1	5"
	#1	10 1/4"
	#2	15 7/8"
	#2	21 3/4"
	#3	28"
	#3	34 3/4"
	#3	41 3/4"
	#4	49 5/8"
	#10 stripping guide	59 5/8"
	#12 stripping guide	71"
9' #5 line	#1	5"
	#1	10 1/4"
	#1	15 1/2"
	#1	21 3/8"
	#1	27 3/8"
	#2	33 3/4"
	#2	40 1/2"
	#3	47 7/8"
	#4	56 1/8"
	#8 stripping guide	67"
	#10 stripping guide	77 1/2"
9' #8 line	#2	5"
	#2	10 1/4"
	#2	15 1/2"
	#3	21 3/8"
	#3	27 3/8"
	#3	33 3/4"
	#3	40 1/2"
	#4	47 7/8"
	#4	56 1/8"
	#10 stripping guide	65 5/8"
	#12 stripping guide	76 1/2"

Taping on Guides

Spine your tip section as you did earlier with your butt section. Wrap a piece of masking tape around the base of your tip section and mark it in line with the soft side. Join your tip and butt sections and lay them on a flat surface. With a piece of chalk, mark the position of each guide on your blank, using a tape measure for reference; the chalk marks should be in line with the soft side on both the tip and butt. Secure your guides over the chalk marks by wrapping a short length of masking tape over one foot of each guide. The guides should be roughly in line with the marks on the soft side of each section.

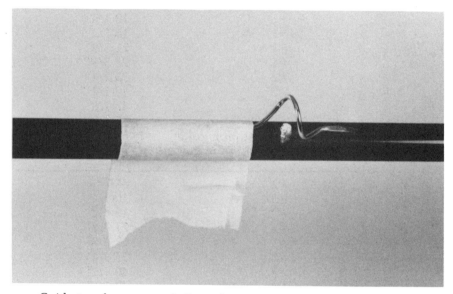

Guide taped on over a chalk mark.

Thread Tension

Resistance is required to execute thread wraps properly. Some fly-fishing mail-order houses offer good thread-tension devices, but setting the spool in a bowl and running the thread through the pages of a thick book also works well.

The author's thread-tension device. (The book is not used for thread-tension here; instead, its weight secures the device.)

Thread Wrapping

Before wrapping, set aside a 6″ to 8″ length of thread, which will later be used as a "tie-off loop" to secure the wrap; fly-line backing works well also. To begin wrapping your guides, hold your butt section horizontal with both hands; palms should be down, thumbs inside pointing together; the guide to be wrapped should be between your hands. Pull enough thread from your tension set-up to reach the guide. Wrap the thread completely around your butt section about 1/8″ to 3/16″ from the guide foot; the thread should come from your tension set-up to the top of your blank. Hold the thread end on the guide's side of the turn and away from the blank. While keeping slight tension on the thread, pull the section toward you an inch or so as the thread slips around it. This will straighten the thread out neatly. Press one thumb against the thread end and slowly rotate the blank, locking the thread end under each new turn of thread. Angle the section slightly so that the turns of thread lay

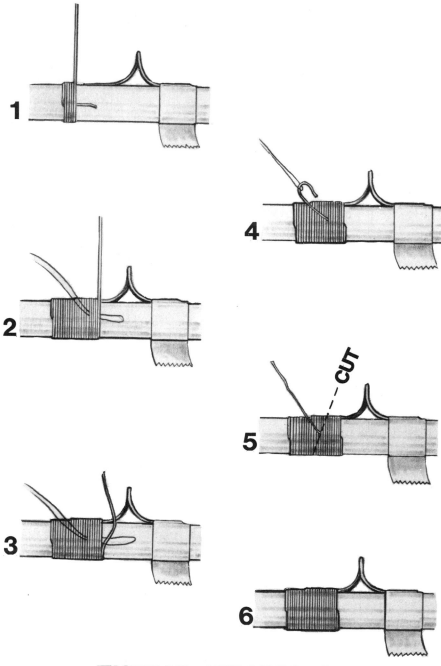

THREAD WRAPPING

up against one another snugly. Continue rotating the section, using thumb pressure to keep the wraps from slipping. You will need to alternate thumbs as the section rotates.

When you have the thread end secured under four or five turns, stop and cut off the thread end close to the wraps. This is easily performed with a pair of fly-tying scissors. As you continue wrapping, stop occasionally to compress the turns of thread with your thumbnail or a plastic spoon. Compress the wrap from the side where the thread is being added—not the side where the thread is locked in. On a typical guide wrap you will want to stop and compress the thread four or five times.

With about 1/8" of wrap left to add, begin wrapping over the center of your tie-off loop keeping the loop on the opposite side of your blank from the guide; the loop end should be away from the wrap. With your wrap finished, hold the last turn in place with your thumb and cut the thread about 2" from the wrap. Put the thread end through your tie-off loop. Pull your tie-off loop back through the last 1/8" of wraps, taking the thread end with it. The thread end is now locked in place.

Next, pull the thread end firmly at a 90° angle to the blank; the last 1/8" of wraps should form a sort of tent. Maintaining tension, slide your fly-tying scissors down the thread and cut close. The thread tent will snap back down, covering the thread end. Should any part of the thread end still project from the wraps, it can be trimmed later during the finish procedures. Remove the masking tape from the other guide foot, turn your section end for end, and repeat the wrapping process. When all the guides are wrapped, you will want to wrap your hookkeeper in the same manner. If you have chosen a loose-ring keeper, a piece of masking tape will keep the ring secured while you wrap. Leave a space of about 1/8" between the edge of your hookkeeper wraps and the edge of your cork grip. Your hookkeeper should be in line with your guides. If your grip is faced with a winding check, simply add a thread wrap from the check to the hookkeeper wrap.

Wrapping the Cork

Lock your thread in against the lower edge of your hookkeeper wrap. Carefully continue wrapping, with light pressure, until you are onto the cork and, finally, about 1/4" up the cork. On grips with only a short lip in front (full Wells, half Wells, and cigar), wrap only a few turns up this lip. Wrap another 1/8" of turns over a loop of rod-winding thread (here it will work better than a loop of backing). Use this loop to pull the thread end through as you did on the guide wraps, but work slowly and gently. Separate the thread slightly on either side of the thread end. Carefully cut off the thread end with a single-edged razor blade. Saw the blade across the thread and against the cork. The steep angle of the thread over the cork prohibits the style of thread-end cutting used previously.

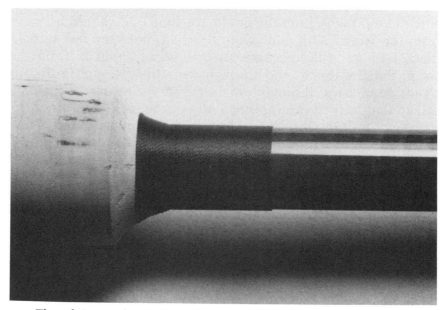

Thread wrapped onto the cork.

The Tip Top

Lightly sand the last 1/2" of your tip at its point with #320 sandpaper for tooth. Test your tip top's fit on your tip. If the fit is loose you may shim by gently filing a small groove in the point of your tip and looping a 6" piece of rod-winding thread over the groove. Simply hold the thread a couple of inches from your tip's point as you push the tip top on. Once you have a good fit, remove the tip top and mix a batch of *fast-cure* epoxy. Work a generous amount of the epoxy inside the tip top's cylinder with a toothpick. Slip your tip top into place and wipe off any excess epoxy with a rag. Sight down your tip, with the guides underneath, and align the tip top with your guides. Fast-cure epoxy is best because it is heat-soluble so you can remove the tip top should it become damaged or worn. If you doubt that your epoxy is heat-soluble, mix a batch and use it to glue a toothpick into a tip top. Once the epoxy has cured, heat the tip top on a range burner and see if the epoxy lets go. You will end up with a ruined tip top, but you will also end up with peace of mind.

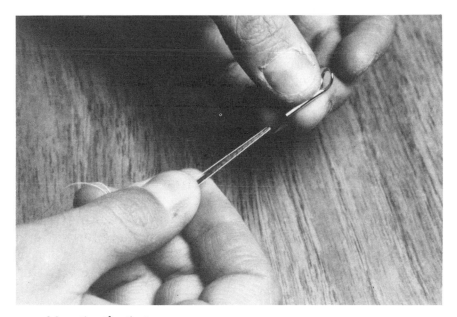

Mounting the tip top.

A wrap next to your tip top will give it a finished look. Start the thread about 1/2″ from your tip top. Wrap to the tip top, then wrap the thread back over itself a few close turns in the opposite direction. Wrap in a tie-off loop and finish as usual. The short double layer of thread makes a visually pleasing transition from the blank to the tip top.

Ferrule Wrapping

A rod's appearance is usually improved with the addition of some kind of ferrule wrap—at least to my eye. On rods with the spigot (plug) ferrule, a wrap of 1/2" to 3/4" on both the male the female stations is a good idea; start the spigot-ferrule wraps within 1/8" of the rims of both sections. On rods with a tip-over-butt ferrule in which a swell or sleeve on the tip slides directly over the butt, you can put a short wrap at the rim of the female ferrule and another where the ferrule swell begins; or you may wrap the full length of the female ferrule.

Decorative Wraps

A diamond wrap is a patterned decorative wrap created by the systematic layering of various colors of rod-winding thread; I don't use diamond wraps on my rods. A fly rod is, in my opinion, too delicate and graceful for such a busy, heavy-looking wrap. My preference is for inlaid turns and thread trim rings.

The Inlaid Turn

Having taken a few turns on your primary thread and having cut off the locked-in thread end, wrap a few more turns over a short (approximately 3") piece of trim thread; only about 3/4" of your trim thread should project from the point it was first

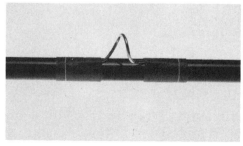

Completed inlaid turns.

wrapped into your primary wrap. When you have added five or six turns of primary thread over your trim thread, closely cut the 3/4″ end off with your fly-tying scissors. Carefully pull on the remaining end of the trim thread until the cut stub disappears completely under the primary wrap. Adjust your blank so your primary thread is just short of lapping again over your trim thread; stop rotating the blank. Holding your blank stationary, bring your trim thread around the blank in the same direction as your primary thread and up against the main wrap. When the trim thread reaches completely around your blank, bring the end of your trim thread over your primary thread, then back under it, and angle the projecting trim thread away from the wrap. As you begin rotating the blank again, you will find that the trim thread completely circles the blank once and that both its ends meet, creating an inlaid turn. I like to have the ends meet in line with the guide feet. After you take a few more turns of primary thread to lock in the inlaid turn, you can use the same piece of trim thread to add another inlaid turn—and still others if you like. You can also take two or more turns of trim thread to widen your inlaid turns.

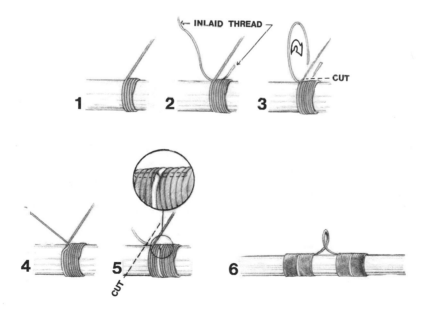

INLAID TURN

Inlaid turns are attractive in guide wraps, ferrule wraps, hookkeeper wraps, and nonfunctional decorative wraps. Inlaid turns can also be attractive in combination with thread trim rings.

Thread Trim Rings

These are simply short thread wraps of about three to eight turns that can dress up a rod elegantly. The trick with thread trim rings is to make the first turn, and all subsequent turns, directly over the tie-off loop; this offers the most control—especially with thread trim rings of five turns or fewer. When you pull the thread end back under your wraps, it will come out the opposite side of the wrap—not between the turns of thread. By wrapping in your tie-off loop slightly farther around your blank than the first thread end, both ends of your thread trim ring will lock up in tightening. Tighten your trim ring by pulling gently on both thread ends; pull the ends to the sides of the blank in line with the direction they leave the trim ring. With a toothpick straighten and even out your thread trim ring; use the toothpick to press the trim ring up against a primary wrap if that is its intended location. Cut off the thread ends by rocking a single-edged razor blade gently against them; be careful not to cut into your blank.

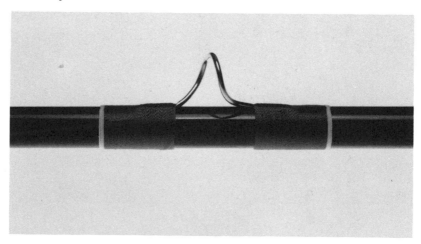

Guide wrap with thread trim rings.

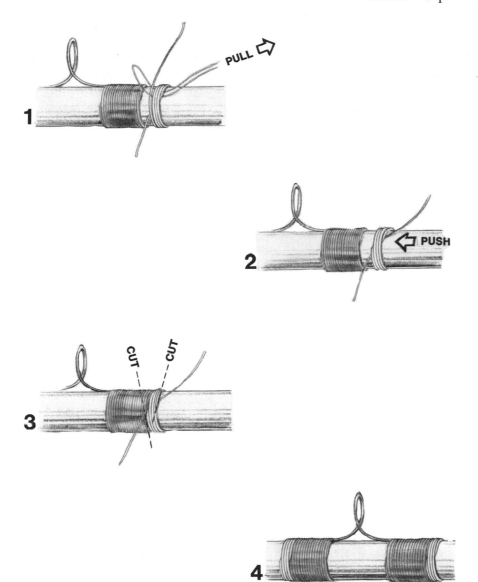

THREAD TRIM RING

Thread trim rings may be of N.C.P. thread, standard thread of a color lighter than your primary wraps, or standard thread of the same color as your primary wraps. To keep thread trim rings and primary wraps of identical color distinct, separate them with space or thread trim rings of another color. By tastefully combining one or more thread colors with inlaid turns and thread trim rings you will find that your fly rod can have an elegant and unique appearance.

5 *Inscription and Finish*

Most anglers like a rod to have some kind of inscription; almost always the length of the rod and its designated line weight or weights are appropriate. You may also want to put your name on the rod as builder and possibly the name of the rod's future owner. Since I build a lot of rods, I have found it helpful to have a serial number on each rod; later, by referring to my notebooks, I can look up any pertinent information should a rod need repair or should someone want another rod just like it.

I use an ink pen and silver Winsor & Newton ink for my inscriptions. Other good inks include black India and water-thinned White-Out: White-Out is actually a correction fluid. My nib (penpoint) is a Hunt Extra-fine Bowl Pointed #512. Russ Peak told me about a silver pencil he found in an art-supply store. I found one very similar, a Berol Prismacolor #949.

Before inscribing the blank, carefully clean the inscription area with a rag and some solvent (acetone, epoxy thinner, or mineral spirits). You will also have to sand the inscription area lightly with #320 sandpaper if you want to use the pencil. Remove all sanding dust with a tack rag before inscribing with the pencil.

Writing on a curved surface is tricky, and more difficult because your hands must not touch the inscription area since

Writing an inscription with a pen.

Completed inscription.

that may impair the finish. To offset these complications, work slowly; practice on another part of the blank or on a scrap section of blank before making your final inscription.

Selecting a Finish

There are many good finishes for rodmaking and most fall into the four categories listed below:

1. Natural varnishes. These can be thinned by putting the varnish into a small container—a film canister, for example—and setting that container into a pan containing a shallow layer of very warm water. Use four to eight thin coats and do not wait too long between coats; the container should have recommended recoating times on it. Pratt and Lambert #51 is an excellent varnish. Some of the natural varnishes sold as "spar" varnish are good, too. While natural varnishes give good performance and can produce a handsome finish, they lack the durability and life span of the urethanes and epoxies.

2. Urethanes. Urethanes are usually thinned with mineral spirits (paint thinner) if thinning is necessary. Three to seven thin coats should do. One excellent urethane is #90 gloss Varathane. Urethanes are tough, flexible, and offer good adhesion. Some, like Varathane #90, have excellent self-leveling properties.

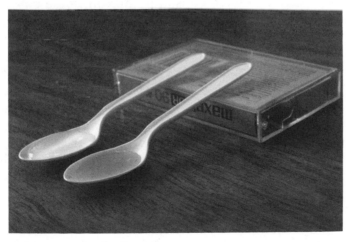

Measuring epoxy in plastic spoons.

3. Epoxies. Of the finishes commonly used in rodmaking, epoxies offer the longest life, greatest durability, and best adhesion; the best epoxies also offer remarkable flexibility—especially in light of their hardness. Hobbypoxy clear two-part epoxy enamel paint (components #HO8 and #HO2) has excellent properties for rodmaking. I mix it thoroughly and let it stand for about one hour before application. Hobbypoxy can be mixed, used, and then stored overnight in a refrigerator for use the next day; two applications of a single mix are all I recommend, however. If you plan to store Hobbypoxy in your refrigerator, be certain to use an airtight container to prevent any escape of vapors.

On the negative side, epoxy finishes can be temperamental regarding temperature, humidity, and mix. Also, epoxy fumes are generally more dangerous than those of the previously mentioned finishes—though all finish and solvent fumes should be controled (see Chapter 9). Nevertheless, with care and patience you can safely produce a handsome epoxy finish.

Hobbypoxy makes a thinner for their finish (#HO7), and thinning can be useful—especially in eliminating bubbles in the first coating. With two-part epoxy finishes, I have always found that using slightly more A (resin) component than B (catalyst) component insures a good cure, free of tackiness—by slightly, I mean that if you can barely perceive that there is more A than B, that is plenty. Of course you can always test whatever epoxy you have chosen by mixing some batches with different ratios of A and B, then seeing how they set up before choosing one for your rod. I have had good results measuring my epoxy with plastic spoons. Set two identical spoons in the same position with their bowls level; you will need to prop their handles with something—a cassette cartridge case works well. Since the bowls are identical in size and shape, you can fill them, one for each component, and compare quantities accurately; use another pair of spoons to pour the components into the first pair. As the plastic spoons may have a chemical reaction with the epoxy, work with at least moderate speed. Hobbypoxy can be flowed on heavier than the previously mentioned finishes so two to four coats should do.

4. Polymers. These are two-part finishes that have become popular with home rod builders. Polymer finishes produce minimal vapors, set up quickly, and build heavily, requiring only one or two coats. If you choose a polymer finish, take care in measuring your mix and stir it slowly and thoroughly. Follow the instructions on the containers and brush slowly as polymers release bubbles grudgingly. Here again, adding slightly more A component than B seems the best way to insure a good cure.

Rotation System

Although you can set your rod in notches cut in a cardboard box and rotate the rod 1/4 turn every few minutes until the finish cures, a much better system combines a rotation device and a cradling device. There are good rotation and cradling devices offered by many fly shops and fly-fishing mail-order houses, but I chose to make my own. My rotation devices incorporate: a *base*, consisting of a short length of 2 × 4; a *plate*, cut from aluminum sheeting and wood-screwed to the base; and a small 6 to 8 R.P.M. *synchronous motor*; you can use faster motors as you improve your skills. If the shaft of the motor is short, I will epoxy on an extension of scrap blank or brass or aluminum tubing. My cradling devices incorporate a short length of 2 × 4 and a couple of castors.

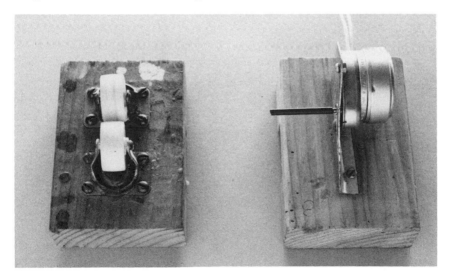

A rotation device and a cradling device.

Finishing

Before finishing it is wise to prepare yourself mentally. Applying the finish is probably the most demanding and critical construction step you must face. This doesn't mean you should panic; it does mean that care and patience will be rewarded. A poor finish is tough to fix and may require a complete redoing; do it right the first time and you will flow through this step with ease.

It is a good idea to practice finishing on wraps made on a section of scrap blank; practice until you are satisfied with the results. Another word of advice, the vapors from your finish are a health hazard; read Chapter 9, on shop safety, and follow its guidelines.

There are two ways to approach finish lines. Most rodmakers run their finish out beyond the edges of each wrap about 1/16" or more; there is nothing wrong with this method: it looks good and has been the standard for many years. I prefer to stop my finish at the exact edges of each wrap for two reasons: first, I think this method offers the easiest, neatest thread-wrapping replacement—when thread wraps need replacement due to worn or damaged guides. Second, I think ending the finish at

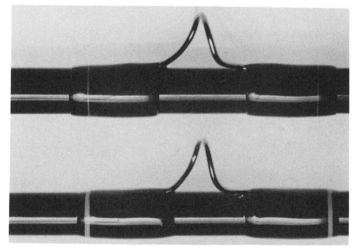

Finish to edge, and past edge of thread wrap.

the edges of a wrap gives the cleanest, most elegant appearance.

Getting a precise finish line isn't as tough as it might seem. Simply apply the finish with extra care and patience at the edges of a wrap. If you run the finish slightly over, it can be cleaned up with a narrow strip of fabric looped over the end of a toothpick. At the worst, you might have to remove the finish with a rag and some solvent.

Begin by attaching the point of your butt section to a rotation device. I use masking tape for this. Use a cradling device to support your butt by its grip. Start your rod rotating. With a brush, begin flowing finish onto a thread wrap; I use disposable brushes made by the Epoxy Coatings Company and sold through many fly-fishing supply outlets. Give all guide and decorative wraps a light, complete coat of finish.

When you get to the inscription, flow finish onto and completely around the blank for the length of the inscription. Smooth out this finish with repeated horizontal brush strokes; each stroke should run the length of the inscription finish. Your brush should barely touch the blank, primarily stroking the finish; any real brush pressure could damage your inscription. Complete your first coat of finish by carefully applying an extra-thin coat to the thread wraps over the end of your cork grip; a heavier coating of finish might result in bubbles caused by air escaping the porous cork. You can stop your finish at the edge of the wrap or run it out slightly onto the cork.

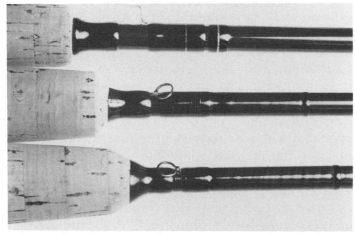

Finish over thread on grip and part way over winding check.

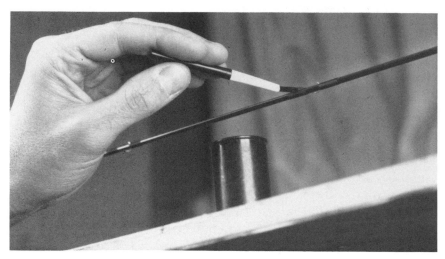

Brushing finish on a guide wrap.

If your thread wraps stop at a winding check, you can simply stop the finish at the edge of the thread. Rubber winding checks seem to last longer if partially covered with finish; do this only with the epoxy and polymer finishes, however, as urethanes and varnishes, due to a chemical reaction with the rubber, may never fully set up.

When your first coat of finish has cured to the proper degree for application of the next coat, you will want to do a little preparation. With a single-edged razor blade gently remove any bumps, thread ends, or bubbles that have formed on your finish. Don't touch the finish with your hands; this could leave oil from your skin and damage the next coating. With a tack rag, or a small piece cut from one, remove any visible dust that has settled on your finish; touch the tack rag to your finish as little and as gently as possible.

Apply your second coat of finish as you did the first—although you may not need to recoat the inscription. As your second coat cures, check occasionally for bubbles, especially at the cork, and pop them with a toothpick.

Continue adding coats of finish, following these guidelines, until you are satisfied. There is no need for a heavy finish; if your finish is level—barely showing, if at all, the texture of the thread—that should be plenty. After giving your finish enough time to cure fully, all that remains is to mount any remaining reel-seat parts with fast-cure epoxy; this will allow access to the inside of the butt for future repairs.

With this your rod is complete, a product of your craftsmanship, taste, determination, and patience. You have earned your reward—the satisfaction of accomplishment.

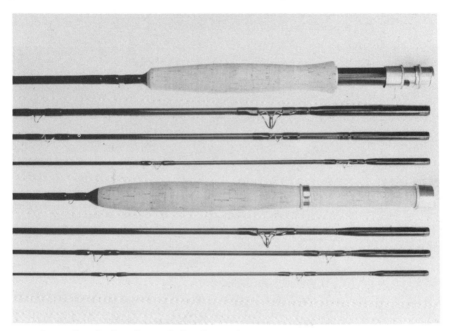

Some finished rods made by the author.

6 Repairs

Every rod you build will potentially need future repairs. If you make rods it is well that you can maintain them.

Guide Replacement

Your most common repair will be replacement of worn or damaged guides. Start by running a single-edged razor blade along the top of the guide foot, cutting through finish and thread. Cut from the end of the foot toward the center of the guide. This procedure is tough on razor blades so I save my used or dull blades for this purpose. Once you have cut the thread from the tops of both feet you can remove the guide with a sharp pull. Next, peel off the cut thread; the finish should hold all the cut thread together so it comes off as a sheet. With a corner of your razor blade work the thread end loose and unwind any remaining thread; the finish should come with it.

With a sharp single-edged razor blade carefully trim down the high points of the finish ridges that formed around each end of each wrap. These needn't be trimmed close; just take the ridges down by one-half to two-thirds. With #220 sandpaper smooth out the fine ridges that formed under the thread; this will make later compression of the wraps easier. A few turns of masking tape will protect the blank as you sand.

Select a new guide the same size and style as the original.

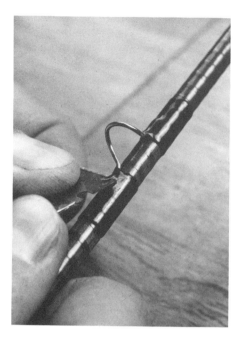

Cutting the finish from the top of a guide foot with a single-edge razor blade.

Peeling off thread wraps.

Dress the feet of the new guide and wrap it on exactly where the old guide was; be certain your wraps cover exactly the same space the original wraps covered—otherwise you may have finish problems later. To complete, coat with finish as usual.

Broken Rod Sections

Broken rod sections, especially tips, are common. Usually the cause is things that shut: house doors, car doors, and trunk lids. Sometimes the angler will break a rod butt by horsing a big fish with the rod bent back at a sharp angle. Whatever the cause, you will first need to determine if repair is practical.

If the break is within the last 12″ of the tip's point, there may be a loss in performance if the tip is repaired. If the break is within the last 5″ or so of the tip's point, cutting the broken edge off and putting a new tip top on what remains may produce a satisfactory (or even improved!) rod. A break really close to a ferrule may prove impractical to repair.

First you must check the break. A clean break can probably be repaired with a sleeve, but splits in the blank longer than an inch offer little hope.

The broken section on the left is a good prospect for repair; the one on the right is hopeless.

If repair looks promising, start by wrapping masking tape around the blank just beyond the end of any splits. The masking tape marks the end of the splits and protects the blank during cutting. Cut the blank against a grinding wheel at the edge of the masking tape. Repeat this procedure on the other broken end. Flatten the cut ends by rotating them against the face of the grinding wheel at a 90° angle. Check the ends thoroughly both inside and out for any sign of splits; if you suspect splits, trim again until you feel certain you are beyond them.

Next, find a section of scrap blank that will fit snugly over the larger-diameter broken piece; the walls of the scrap should be at least as thick as the walls of your blank. I like a section to fit a distance of about five times its outside diameter into the scrap section. Trim the scrap, if necessary, to obtain this depth. With a strip of #220 sandpaper looped over a stick, thoroughly score the inside of the scrap blank; also with #220 sandpaper, sand the finish from the part of the larger-diameter broken piece that fits into the sleeve. Slide the scrap section on again. Mark with chalk the broken piece at the point where the scrap section stops. If the chalk mark is beyond the five-diameter point, trim the scrap section appropriately. Cut the scrap section about ten diameters up from its base. Take a last look down the scrap section and if the inside walls are not thoroughly scored from end to end, make sure they are.

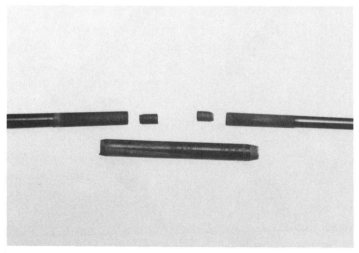

A broken section—end plugs and a sleeve ready to glue up.

Remove all the guides and finish from the smaller-diameter broken piece and sand the finish from its base, where it will mount in the scrap sleeve, with #220 sandpaper, until all the finish is removed. Slide this piece, point first, into the base of the scrap section. If you are lucky, the broken piece will stop snugly with its base half way up the scrap section. If the broken piece slides in beyond this point, you will have to shim. To shim, mount this broken piece in your rotation system and start all turning. Brush out an even layer of slow-cure epoxy, thinned under a heat lamp, over the sanded area; use only enough heat to thin the epoxy slowly and no more. The next day you can mount the broken piece in your turning system and dress the epoxy with sandpaper or files (see Chapter 7 on dressing with files) until your broken piece fits the correct depth into your scrap section sleeve. Remove a little at a time and test fit frequently.

Score the *inside* of both broken pieces where they fit into the scrap sleeve. Find a piece of scrap blank that fits inside the repair end of the larger-diameter broken piece and another that fits inside the repair end of the smaller-diameter broken piece; these scrap pieces should fit in point first. Sand the scrap blank pieces to bare graphite, then cut them so they fit inside the broken pieces about 1/4" to 1/2". Glue the scrap into the broken pieces with slow-cure epoxy.

The next day, cut off any scrap blank that is extending from the broken pieces against a grinding wheel. Flatten the repair end of the broken pieces against the wheel. To minimize stress, round the edges of the broken pieces to about 1/8" from their rims at their repair ends.

Prepare the sleeve by dressing both its edges to a long (1/4" to 3/8") taper against a grinding wheel. Smear a thin layer of slow-cure epoxy over the last 3" of the smaller-diameter broken piece. Slide the sleeve onto this broken piece with a slow, twisting motion; the sleeve should stop with the broken piece's base about halfway up it.

Using a rag, wipe any epoxy off the broken piece above the sleeve—a little solvent may help. Smear some more slow-cure epoxy inside the sleeve and on the sanded area of the larger-diameter broken piece. Twist this piece as you slowly push it halfway up the sleeve and, again, wipe off any excess epoxy. As the epoxy cures, you can periodically sight down the section and, if there is any play at all, adjust for straightness.

The next day you will want to reinforce the sleeve with wrappings of fiberglass. Secure the end of a fiberglass strand a couple of inches away from the sleeve with masking tape. Make a few wide spirals of the glass until you reach the sleeve, then cover the full length of the sleeve with close turns. If the sleeve is on a butt section, you will need two layers of glass; on a tip, one layer should be plenty. To finish, wrap the glass strand away from the sleeve in about 2" of wide spirals and secure with a piece of masking tape. Cut the glass strand past the tape.

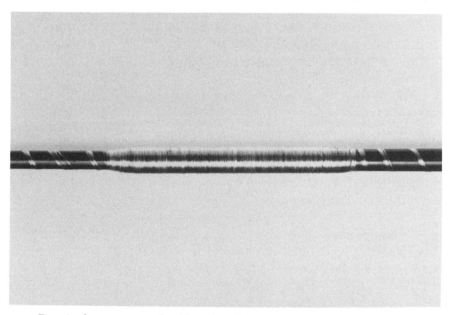

Repair sleeve wrapped with a fiberglass strand.

Put the section into your rotation system and start things turning. With a brush, brush handle, or Popsicle stick, gently work a thin layer of slow-cure epoxy out over the full length of the sleeve; thin the epoxy with a heat lamp, using as little heat as possible. Work the epoxy to a smooth taper at the ends of the sleeve. Once the epoxy has really saturated the glass fibers, turn off the heat lamp and let the section rotate overnight.

The next day you can dress the hardened epoxy in your turning system. The best approach is to start with a couple of

10″ mill bastard files (see Chapter 7 on dressing blanks) and follow with #220 sandpaper; or you can, instead, dress the epoxy with #100 sandpaper, followed by #220 sandpaper.

Adding epoxy to glass wraps on a repair sleeve.

Dressing a butt section with a pair of 10″ mill bastard files—the same process used to dress a repair sleeve.

Dress only enough to level the epoxy and smooth out the end tapers. When this is done, wrap the repair with thread (perhaps a thread similar in color to the blank) and coat with finish as usual.

Cork Grips

Damaged cork grips are common, and their repair requires more labor than most anglers expect. To repair a cork grip you must remove the hookkeeper and all the guides from the butt section, dress off the old grip (or at least the part of it that is damaged), rebuild the grip, and replace the hookkeeper and guides. Use your turning system to spin the butt as you dress off the old grip with a Dremel tool or #80 sandpaper; leave a little cork around the blank to insure you do not nick or damage the surface of the blank. If you decide to leave part of the original grip, be certain you have a flat, smooth surface for the new corks to meet.

Reel Seats

Reel seats should only be replaced as a last resort. Damaged cork-and-slide-band reel seats can simply be dressed off in your turning system; then the corks for a new cylinder can be glued on from the base of your butt section. All-metal and wood-filler seats are another matter.

A properly mounted all-metal or wood-filler seat cannot be removed from the blank; the blank will have to be cut just above the old seat, using a grinding wheel. This, of course, means part of the grip must be removed for blank access. To turn the new grip the guides will have to be removed, otherwise they will cause oscillation when rotating at high speed. As you can see, most reel seats are mounted for keeps.

If you do have to cut off a reel seat, you'll need to reinforce the remaining base of your butt section with epoxy and fiberglass twine (see Chapter 2 on reinforcing the blank for a fighting butt), then a snug-fitting section of scrap blank must be epoxied inside to form an extension. The extension need only fit 2″ or 3″ up the blank and the fiberglass reinforcing should cover all this. Sand the inside of the blank's base to remove any parting compound and sand the surface of the scrap blank for tooth.

Thankfully, reel-seat replacement is rarely mandatory and most repairs are relatively easy and provide good results.

7 Advanced Techniques

Up to this point we have, for the most part, approached home rodmaking within conventional parameters. This chapter, however, is clearly aimed at the adventurous—you may explore as little or as deeply as you choose the fascinating realm of fly-rod design and action.

The techniques covered in this chapter are more or less the product of rodmaker Russ Peak. Russ kindly shared with me the basic principles and I, in turn, worked out the details. I now give to you, in one chapter, all the information I can; but you too may have to work out some details.

Stripping Finish

Developing your own blanks will require that you remove the original finish from your rod sections. This is accomplished with an epoxy-and-paint stripper: a paste or liquid that softens the finish. The resulting sludge can be scrapped off with the back side of a knife blade—the sharp side could cut into the blank. Remove any remaining finish with steel wool. Observe safety precautions when using the stripper (see Chapter 9).

Dressing Ridges from Rod Shafts

Some manufacturers do not sand off the spiral ridges left by the shrink tape during production. These should be dressed off using files. I used to start this operation with a pair of vixen files—and vixen files are expensive. To obtain my first pair I purchased one damaged file at a reduced price and halved it. But this required a couple of long weeks and left little doubt in my mind that a good file is indeed hard. But you do not need vixen files, nor do I use them anymore. Russ Peak called me as this book was being prepared, to tell me that a pair of 10″ mill bastard files will perform as well as, yet cost less than, the vixens. Prepare the mill bastard files by briefly working all four corners against a grinding wheel; this will remove any burrs from the edges of the files. All new files used for rod work should be dressed in this manner.

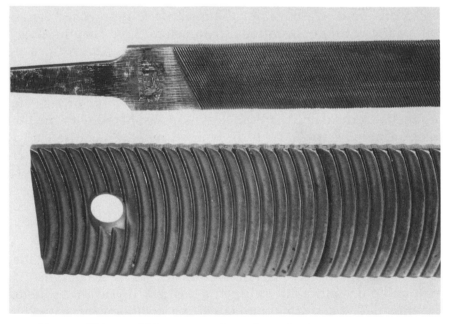

Top: a mill bastard file. *Bottom:* the wide teeth of a vixen file.

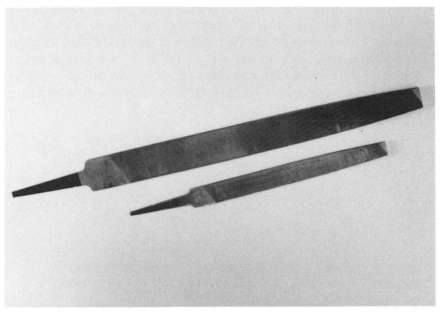

An 8″ and a 10″ mill file.

To dress the ridges from a rod section, mount the section in your turning system without employing a support. Hold the files in one hand with the teeth in the correct cutting direction; one file should be on top of the blank, the other underneath. Work the files down the section at about a 45° angle to the section. Steadying the spinning section with your other hand, remove only a little material at a time and stop to inspect your progress frequently. When the ridges are almost gone, switch to a pair of 8″ mill bastard files and continue in the same manner. Stop using the files when all that remains of the ridges are a few dark spots, then give the shaft a quick once over with #220 sandpaper and finish with a brief sanding with #320.

The Brush Finish

A complete refinish is required as a final step in most rods with modified or custom actions. However, some rod makers may want to use a brush finish on their rods without altering rod action; for this reason I will cover the brush finish first.

A brush finish, by my definition, describes a finish hand-brushed onto both the thread wrappings and rod-shaft surfaces. Brushing finish over rod-shaft surfaces is quite a different proposition from over the thread wraps only, as we discussed in Chapter 5. A brush finish not only offers a unique appearance, it can also be reapplied, at any time, resulting in a rod that looks like new.

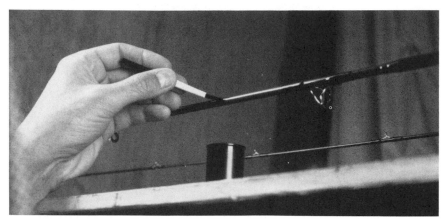

Brush-finishing a rod section.

You can use any of the finishes described in Chapter 5 except, perhaps, the polymer. My experience indicates the polymers are too thick for brush finishing, but I haven't tried them all nor have I spent a great deal of time with polymers, so I won't rule them out absolutely.

You must put a primary foundation coating on the rod shafts before adding thread wrappings—this protects the shafts from wearing against the guide feet. You can brush a thin coating out that covers each section completely, or just add finish at each guide location; either way, leave the male ferrule station of the butt unfinished to a point about 1/4" below the rim of the female ferrule. Even when the entire brush finish is complete, this area should remain bare.

Lightly sand this foundation coating, then add all thread wraps and the inscription; give the thread wraps two or three thin coats of finish. You can either wait for the guide coatings to cure, then sand them lightly with your finger tips and some dry pumice powder, or you can add the final coatings while the guide coatings are still tacky; either way, you will want to clean all sanded finish and bare graphite with thinner or solvent before brushing out the final coatings. You will need at least two complete coatings on the rod shafts to provide adequate protection: if your foundation coating was complete, not just at the guide locations, you can count this as a complete coating. You will have to experiment to determine the variables: number of coatings, thinning, finish type, and so forth.

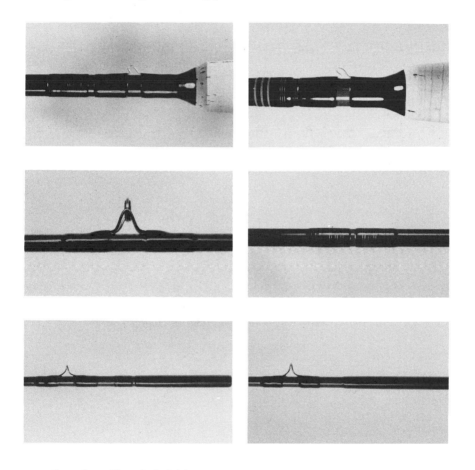

Samples of brush-finishing.

The principles of brush finishing are simple: get the finish on a section between two thread wraps (between two guides, a guide and a ferrule, and the like) then smooth and even the finish with long brush strokes; it is all technique. Russ holds his sections as he brushes; I mount mine in my turning system at 4 to 10 R.P.M.s. Whichever approach you use, plenty of practice on scrap sections is time well invested.

Tip and Butt Cutting

Altering the actions of factory rod shafts is the first step in creating your own actions. The simplest way to alter action is to shorten the tip, butt, or both. Do this with caution. Some blanks will improve, others will diminish in performance, still others will merely change. Thoroughly test cast a blank with the tip top on the point of the tip, then with the tip top secured, with masking tape, at various locations below the point, before deciding whether or not to cut.

Test-Casting Aids

Russ Peak devised a clever temporary grip and reel seat for test casting. It consists of a grip and inexpensive reel seat on a short section of large-diameter fiberglass scrap shafting; the ends of the scrap are notched and a few turns of masking tape at both ends of this assembly will secure it to a blank. I developed a

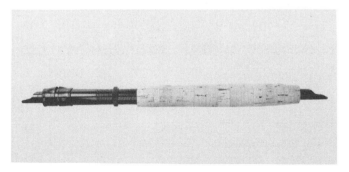

Russ Peak's temporary grip and reel seat—a good use for throwaway cork.

quick, simple method for attaching temporary guides. Guides are mounted onto a thin-walled fiberglass section, then the section is cut up so that each guide is mounted on a short length of blank; a number is inscribed and protected with a spot of finish on each temporary guide; guides are numbered sequentially in order of diameter. Simply slide the guides onto the blank and secure with a light pressure fit.

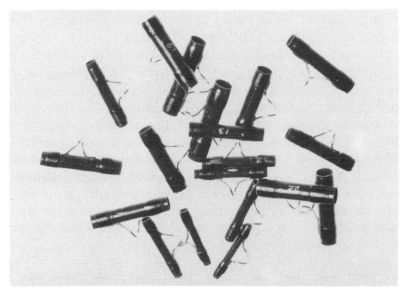

Press-on temporary guides.

Dressing Factory Blanks to Vary Action

You can alter the action of factory blanks by mounting the sections in your turning system and dressing off graphite with a pair of 10″ mill bastard files and sandpaper, as described earlier in this chapter for dressing the ridges from blanks, but really thin-walled sections should be dressed little, if at all. Dressing the tip will make the blank faster; dressing the butt will make the blank slower. Remove the most graphite at the point of the tip and progressively less to the female ferrule—where no material should be removed. On the butt it is the same principle in reverse—with the most material removed at the base and progressively less up to the ferrule.

Creating Blanks

The last technique involves combining various tips and butts to create your own unique fly-rod actions. After stripping the finish, and dressing down the spiral ridges if the factory left them unsanded, you will need to determine the point where the tip and butt meet for ideal energy transfer: the point where the tip and butt are identical in stiffness. Russ and I refer to this as the ferrule point. A temporary juncture can be made by overlapping the sections and securing them with two tight bands of masking tape about 3″ apart. If the tip and butt are a good combination, and if they are joined at the correct ferrule point, the resulting mockup rod should cast a smooth line with a well-formed loop with no shock waves, provided you are a smooth caster. It is vital you develop a smooth, efficient casting technique for rod testing. It is also vital that you extensively test any butt and tip combination, moving the ferrule point repeatedly until you are confident of ideal energy transfer. If you are uncertain, set the sections aside and try it again another day. A windless day is essential, as is patience.

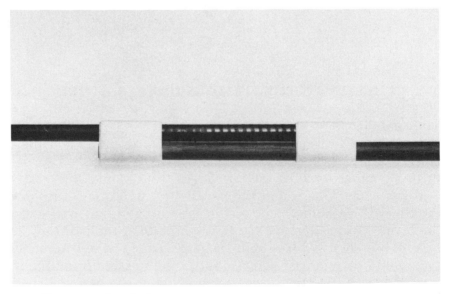

Temporary ferrule juncture.

To combine various tips and butts you will need to make your own ferrules. I feel that the sleeve ferrule is the strongest and have always used it with graphite rod shafts. It is made from a piece of scrap graphite rod shaft that is equal or greater in wall thickness than either the tip or butt at the ferrule point. I like the tip and butt to fit inside the finished sleeve ferrule at a depth of at least five times the maximum inside diameter of the ferrule. If the butt is larger in diameter, at the ferrule point, than the tip, you will have to shim the base of the tip with a layer of heat-lamp-thinned slow-cure epoxy dressed in your turning system to fit.

If the tip is larger, you will need to bore the point of the sleeve with a Dremel tool and a grinding bit; this will require a sleeve with enough wall thickness to allow for the removal of material. The base of the tip is then dressed to flat (no taper) to fit into the bored sleeve. A short piece of graphite scrap is epoxied inside the base of the tip for reinforcement; this scrap should extend about 3/4" beyond the point of the sleeve. Round the rim of the tip's base, to distribute stress better.

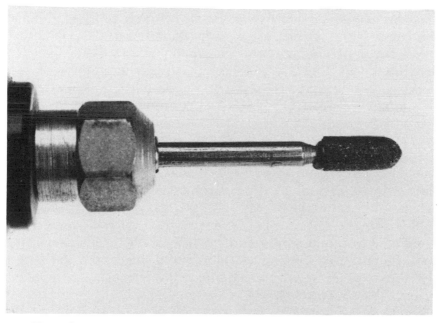

Dremel grinding bit.

Boring Ferrule sleeve with grinding bit.

Whenever you epoxy inside graphite shafting, you must first thoroughly sand the inside walls with strips of sandpaper looped over a short section of scrap blank because the factories use a parting compound between mandrel and blank for easy separation; an adhesion-resistant parting compound will not bond with your epoxy.

There is always the chance that your butt and tip—by nothing less than a miracle—share the same outside diameter at the ferrule point. In this case, no shimming or boring is necessary.

If the sleeve and the point of your butt section do not share the same taper, you will have to make adjustments. With the butt stripped to bare graphite, sand its last couple of inches at the point lightly and evenly with #400 sandpaper. Twist the butt inside the sleeve. Upon removal, the butt will show darkened or shiny areas—these indicate contact between sleeve and butt. Sand these "high spots" with #320, then sand the entire male ferrule lightly with #400 and retest. Repeat until contact is well distributed.

All ferrules should have a space between tip and butt to allow for wear and seating of the male ferrule; I call this a "gap." To adjust the gap, slide the sleeve into place on your tip.

With a scrap section, check the depth of the tip inside the sleeve against the depth of the male ferrule. Trim the tip of the butt so that a 1/4″ gap is left inside the sleeve between the point of the butt and the base of the tip when the sections are joined.

The techniques for epoxying your sleeve in place will vary, depending upon how the sleeve was fit to the tip. Always use slow-cure epoxy for ferrules. For a sleeve that started out equal or larger in diameter than the base of the tip, you will slide the sleeve over the point of the tip and down into place. The epoxy will distribute best if you smear it on the lower 6″ of the tip's base; slowly twist the sleeve as you slide it into place, then wipe the excess epoxy off the tip. Wipe the epoxy from the inside of the sleeve, beyond the tip's base, with strips of fabric looped over a short scrap section.

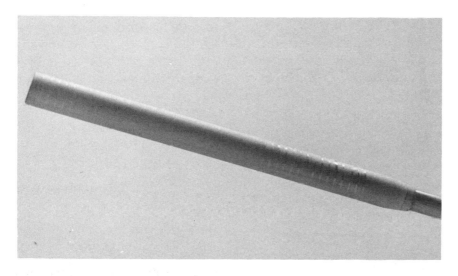

Epoxied-on ferrule sleeve.

Ferrules in which the sleeve was bored to fit the base of the tip require a different technique. Smear a layer of epoxy inside the point of the sleeve and on the base of the tip. Slowly push and twist the tip, base first, into the point of the ferrule sleeve. Remove all epoxy from the inside of the sleeve, beyond the base of the tip, with strips of fabric looped over a scrap section.

Next you must laminate your sleeve with turns of fiberglass. With the sleeve securely mounted and the epoxy cured, mount a short piece of scrap section into the open end of your sleeve with a light pressure fit. Wrap a strand of fiberglass over itself—as you would start a thread wrap—about 1/8″ in front of your sleeve. Wrap the glass, in close turns, to the end of the sleeve. Follow this with a few wide spirals of glass down the scrap piece. Secure the glass strand to the scrap with masking tape; trim the end of the glass strand (for a really heavy-duty rod or the butt ferrule on a four-piece rod, use two layers of glass). A good source for glass is fiberglass cloth, sold in many hardware stores; simply strip a strand from the edge of the cloth.

Apply slow-cure epoxy to the glass wraps; thin the epoxy with the beam from a heat lamp, using as little heat as possible. The glass will become transparent as the epoxy saturates it, leaving only a few highlights of white. Run the epoxy out to about 1/16″ short of the rim of the sleeve and make sure no epoxy seeps in between the sleeve and scrap section. When the epoxy has cured hard, dress it in your turning system using files and sandpaper. Trim the edge of your ferrule against a grinding wheel.

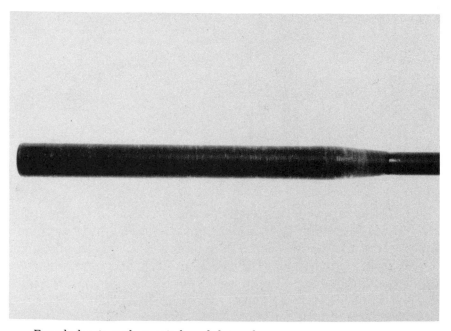

Ferrule laminated, epoxied, and dressed.

For a final fit test, join tip and butt and, while holding your thumb lightly against the lower rim of your sleeve ferrule, shake the blank a few times to see if you feel a "knock"; a knock indicates an improper fit. Adjust the fit as before and trim the butt's point if needed to maintain proper gap. Put your blank up into a mock-up rod and test cast again. If energy transfer is off, dress the tip or butt accordingly. From this point, continue construction of your rod as usual and end with a brush finish.

The techniques in this chapter offer you great scope—you can be not only a rod builder but also a true rod *designer*. Use what you like; the doors are open.

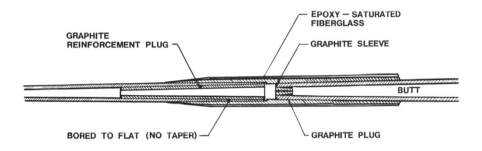

CUTAWAY OF FERRULE BORED FOR LARGE DIAMETER TIP

8 *Principles of Rod Design*

Fly fisherman seem largely unaware of the complexities of fly-rod design. Most imagine that all fly rods possess identical internal tapers and "straight" actions: stiffening steadily and uniformly from point to butt end. This leaves only variations in wall thickness to account for the many different fly-rod actions available on the market.

This frequently held image is grossly simplistic and far from accurate. In the first place, hollow graphite rodshafts are formed on steel mandrels that are available in a great variety of tapers and diameters; some, called variable-taper mandrels, will change tapers at one or more points throughout their length. In the second place, since the shape cut from the graphite sheeting during fabrication also determines a rod's action, only a straight-sided triangular pattern wrapped on a straight-taper mandrel will produce the progressive steady tip-to-butt stiffening most anglers visualize, and in many rods the cutting pattern is much more complex than this.

To further complicate matters, the mandrel designs and cutting patterns used in the tip section may, when compared to those used in the butt section of the same rod, be in sharp contrast.

The author inspecting one manufacturer's selection of tapered rod-shaft-making mandrels. *Courtesy LCI Excelon*

Clearly, the fly-rod designer must work with a great many variables. Manufacturers spend considerable time and money designing their fly rods, so it is no wonder that such things as mandrels and cutting patterns are considered guarded information. Over the years I have developed a relationship with my manufacturers that allows me to experiment with rodshafts fabricated to my specifications. This is uncommon, however, and for most rod builders to expect anything similar is virtually hopeless. On the brighter side, there are now a lot of good rod sections available for the home rod builder to work with, and with the techniques covered in this book, the possibilities are limitless.

Before we investigate the principles of rod design, it will first be helpful to understand, and visualize, how rodshafts are fabricated. To begin, a specific pattern is cut from resin-impregnated graphite sheeting. This pattern will have at least one straight edge that is heat tacked to a tapered steel mandrel. The sheeting is then rolled onto the mandrel under pressure and, because the resins are tacky, everything stays tightly rolled. Next, a special shrink tape is tightly spiraled over the sheeting and tied off securely. This combination of mandrel, shrink tape, and resin-impregnated sheeting is then baked until the resins

Measuring the graphite tape to mark the cutting pattern. *Courtesy LCI Excelon*

Cutting the pattern from the graphite tape. *Courtesy LCI Excelon*

Heat-tacking a graphite pattern to a mandrel. *Courtesy LCI Excelon*

The pressure-rolling table. *Courtesy LCI Excelon*

flow, the shrink tape contracts, and the resins finally harden. All that is left is to remove the mandrel, strip the shrink tape, and trim the section. At this point, the manufacturer may choose to sand off the ridges created by the spiraled shrink tape and coat the shaft with finish, although some manufacturers simply leave the ridges intact and skip the finishing altogether.

Wrapping the graphite with shrink tape. *Courtesy LCI Excelon*

The result of this fabrication is a rodshaft with specific characteristics determined primarily by the cutting pattern and mandrel design; variations in both manufacturing techniques and materials will also exert some influence.

In Chapter 1 we discussed fly-rod action in the general terms fast, slow, and moderate. These actions may be further divided into the categories of straight action and compound action. Straight action means that the rod becomes progressively and consistently stiffer moving from point to butt (Fig. 1). Compound actions do not increase steadily in stiffness. A compound-action rod may stiffen steadily for the first couple of feet from its point and then change suddenly to a slower rate of stiffening (Fig. 1); this may change again at the ferrule and possibly again somewhere in the butt section. In fact, the rate of stiffness increase may change in the rod at any point.

The stiffness of any rod section depends upon its diameters and wall thickness. Graphite rodshafts are tubular structures: the larger the diameter of a tube, the stiffer it becomes. Thickening the walls of a tube will also increase its stiffness. Conversely, reducing the diameter or thinning the walls of a tube make it more pliant.

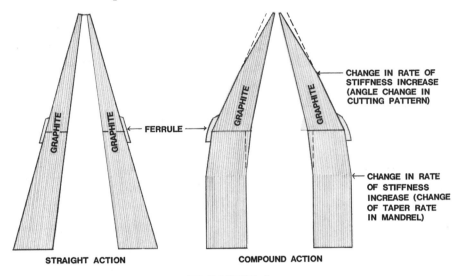

FERRULE

CHANGE IN RATE OF STIFFNESS INCREASE (ANGLE CHANGE IN CUTTING PATTERN)

CHANGE IN RATE OF STIFFNESS INCREASE (CHANGE OF TAPER RATE IN MANDREL)

STRAIGHT ACTION　　　　COMPOUND ACTION

FIGURE 1

The relationship between butt stiffness and tip stiffness is critical to understanding rod action. We have discussed butt stiffness with regards to rod action; however, butt stiffness is best measured by comparing it with tip stiffness.

To clarify how tip stiffness is achieved and how it affects butt stiffness, let's design a rod with two tips and only one butt. To make one tip stiffer than the other, we will form these tips on two different mandrels. To insure that our two tips have identical scale weights, we will cut identical patterns from the graphite sheeting for their construction (Fig. 2).

Tip A will be the stiffer of the two. Tip A is formed on mandrel A, which has a fairly slow taper. Tip B will be formed on mandrel B, which has a faster taper. Both mandrels have identical diameters at their bases, but since mandrel A has a slower taper, it will have a larger diameter at its point. Since larger diameters mean greater stiffness, tip A will be stiffer than

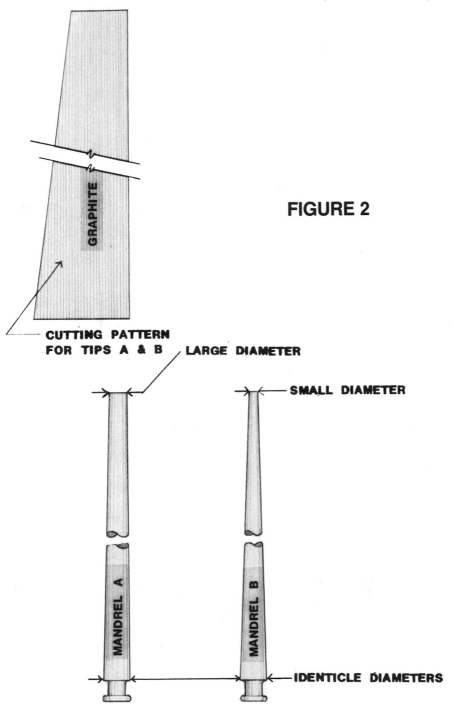

FIGURE 2

GRAPHITE

CUTTING PATTERN
FOR TIPS A & B   LARGE DIAMETER

SMALL DIAMETER

MANDREL A

MANDREL B

IDENTICLE DIAMETERS

tip B overall, yet both will possess identical power at the ferrule point since the diameters there, and the graphite patterns, are identical.

The rods that will result from combining our single butt section with tips A and B will be as follows: with tip A we will have a slow-action rod for, say, a #7 line; with tip B the overall power will drop and the action will speed up, resulting in a moderate-action rod for a #6 line. The stiffer tip A adds to the stiffness of the rod overall, hence the heavier line weight, but this stiffness in the tip drives the flex deeper into the butt, hence the slower action.

If we were to run this same experiment with one tip and two butt sections of contrasting stiffness—yet identical in weight and matching in power at the ferrule point—the results would be much the same. In the same manner that tip stiffness affects butt stiffness, butt stiffness affects tip stiffness.

Just as tip stiffness is a critical rod-design factor so, too, is tip weight. To illustrate, let's make another pair of tips for a single butt section; these we will call tips C and D. Both tips will have identical flex curves on a static deflection board when loaded with identical weights, but the two tips will possess contrasting scale weights.

To create such tips we will need two different mandrels. Tip C will be the lightweight tip and will result from a relatively slim graphite pattern wrapped on mandrel C, which has quite large diameters. Since tip D will be the heavier tip, it will result from a wider graphite pattern wrapped on mandrel D, which has small diameters. If we use the same graphite pattern on both mandrels, C and D, tip D will be much more supple than tip C due to its smaller diameters. So we increase the width of tip D's pattern to add graphite until tip D matches the stiffness of tip C. In adding graphite to tip D we also add weight (Fig. 3).

The rod resulting from the combination of tip C and our butt section will have a relatively fast action and will respond quickly to a casting motion imparted to the butt. In other words, tip C has little mass and therefore little inertia for our butt section to overcome. Tip D, being heavier, has more mass and therefore more inertia to overcome; so when the caster makes a stroke, the butt must flex more to force tip D to respond. This

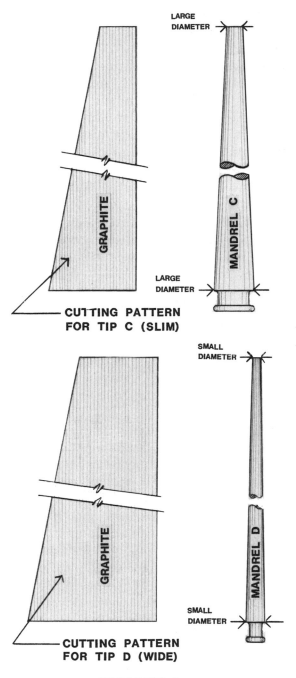

LARGE
DIAMETER

GRAPHITE

MANDREL C

LARGE
DIAMETER

CUTTING PATTERN
FOR TIP C (SLIM)

SMALL
DIAMETER

GRAPHITE

MANDREL D

SMALL
DIAMETER

CUTTING PATTERN
FOR TIP D (WIDE)

FIGURE 3

means, simply, that the rod resulting from our butt combined with tip D will have a slower action than the rod resulting from our butt combined with tip C.

The principles of tip weight cannot really be reversed regarding butt weight. Remember, a caster is swinging a rod tip several feet from his or her hand; the leverage magnifies any weight. Conversely, the rod butt is closer to the hand so it has considerably less leverage, and, because the hand is also a fulcrum, the butt travels a shorter distance than the tip and never reaches the tip's speed during a casting stroke. For all these reasons, the tip, more than the butt, determines the feeling of lightness, or lack of it, in a rod, especially when the rod is cast. It is worth remembering that when most anglers discuss the weight of a rod they are actually responding to both its scale weight and its feeling of weight—the latter being determined primarily by the tip.

Rod designers often use the terms "thin-walled" and "thick-walled" to describe rod sections. These terms mean just what they imply: a thin-walled section is composed of relatively little graphite, gaining its rigidity from its large diameters; a thick-walled section is slender and depends upon its greater quantity of graphite to provide stiffness. Clearly these are relative terms and many rod sections fall in between these two extremes.

My experience indicates that most anglers prefer a rod that feels light. Why, then, would I choose to design rods with thicker-walled sections? For one thing, there are anglers who simply prefer the *feel* of thick-walled rods. More important, however, is the fact that extremely thin-walled sections may lack power, tend toward tip wobble, and be highly susceptible to breakage. This lack of power Russ refers to as "fade," simply meaning that a section runs out of backbone—the harder the angler punches a cast the more the rod's ability to transfer that energy to the line diminishes. "Tip wobble," another Peak term, is also a common problem with very thin-walled sections, especially in longer rods. Tip wobble is just what it sounds like—the tip wobbles during and after the cast. Shortening the rod will sometimes cure this. Because the last characteristic, breakage, is strongly related to wall thickness, the rod designer must also consider how the finished rod will be used, and the client's temperament.

But thin-walled sections also have advantages. They are lighter, recover faster, and are more sensitive than thick-walled sections. The wall thickness of a section is really determined by the intended use, action, length, and intended line size for the finished rod, along with the personal tastes of its future owner. If, for example, a section lacks needed power but has the proper flex, substitute instead a section that is thicker-walled but slimmer. If a rod feels too weighty, try a thinner-walled tip with larger diameters. If the tip wobbles, throwing unwanted waves into the line, try a slightly thicker-walled tip of slimmer profile, or shorten the tip at its point, or shorten the whole rod, or forget the approach you have taken and start completely over!

This is the way a fine rod design is evolved—*empirically*. The challenge is not simply to create a rod that fills some technical goal of making maximum use of a material, but a rod that feels alive in the angler's hand and performs the varied chores of a day's fishing gracefully, efficiently, and pleasingly. Human nature complicates the issue: we all share it, yet it manifests itself in each of us uniquely. Although Russ and I are constantly working with figures and calculations, they are responding to our direction. No number on a sheet of paper is telling us how to suit our next fly rod to human nature; that comes from experience, experimentation, and to a large degree, intuition.

9 *Shop Safety*

I could not write this book in sound conscience if it did not discuss safety considerations. At little expense you can greatly increase the protection of your hands, eyes, and lungs, and provide yourself with safety equipment that can aid in a multitude of other tasks and projects: house painting, furniture repair, cabinet making, and antique restoration to name only a few.

Protective gloves are wise for finish stripping, finishing, and working with your turning system. Gloves for finish stripping and finishing should be leak-proof to protect skin from contact with finishes and solvents. Gloves for your turning system should be heavy enough to protect your hands from cuts and gouges, but, to keep from catching on spinning rod shafts, should also be relatively frictionless. A good fit is essential for maximum protection. Safety gloves come in a variety of types and each is designed for a specific type of exposure; more information can be obtained through a reputable safety-supply outlet and the sources listed at the end of this chapter.

Safety goggles will protect your eyes from finish stripper, finish spills, and from material your turning system may throw. Here again, select carefully as there are a variety of styles. Goggles should be ANSI (American National Standards Institute) certified.

Good ventilation, especially with the more toxic finishes and solvents, is a must. I have done some research on ventilation over the years, but to insure the most accurate up-to-date information I contacted an expert—Angela Babin, Director of the Art Hazards Information Center in New York City. She recommended a window exhaust fan to provide dilution ventilation. The fan should be blocked in the window so that contaminated air cannot seep back into the room around the sides of the fan. Air to replace that which the fan has discharged, called make-up air, should come from an area well away from the fan's exhaust; an open window on the opposite side of the building is good.

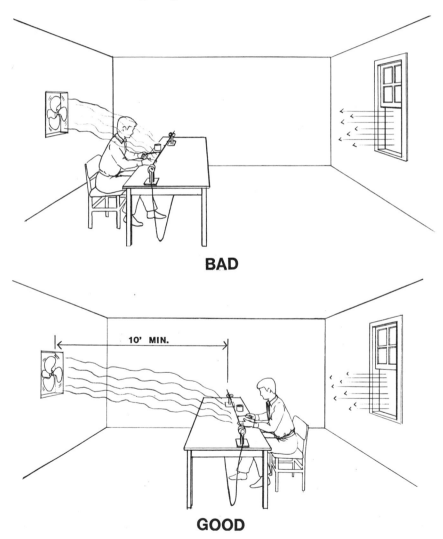

BAD

GOOD

Angela recommends the fan be explosion-proof if it will be within ten feet of solvents, electrical machinery, or any other flammable storage. You would be wise to check your local city fire laws to find out the required placement distance if your fan is not explosion-proof. She says the fan should remain in operation as the finish cures. Position yourself between your fan and your source of make-up air, with your work between you and the fan; this way the vapors are pulled away from you and the make-up air is pulled toward you.

I strongly suggest you consider purchasing a respirator, especially if you plan to work with the more toxic finishes and solvents. Respirators will serve a variety of uses and are reasonably priced. Respirators made by various manufacturers will differ in design; this means that almost anyone can find a respirator that fits. There are several standard tests that will insure a proper fit; if you purchase your respirator at a safety-supply store they can test the fit there. Respirator cartridges are of many types, each with a specific use; when you purchase yours, be certain they will handle your needs. The containers your finish and solvent come in should list hazards; but you should request a material safety data sheet (MSDS) from the manufac-

The author's respirator with cartridges and snap-on dust filters.

turer for each of your solvents and finishes; these sheets will provide much useful information on the hazards and safety procedures pertaining to your products. Most respirators will also protect your lungs from airborne graphite and cork dusts; all you need are the appropriate dust filters.

Reasonable protection and safety habits are easy; the rewards are good health and a comfortable, pleasant rodmaking experience.

Information on safety can be obtained from the following sources:

Art Hazards Information Center
5 Beekman Street
New York, NY 10038
   This valuable information source can also supply the book *Ventilation: A Practical Guide* (Nick Lyons Books), a straight-forward guide to ventilation with lots of information pertinent to the rodmaker's workshop.

Committee on Industrial Ventilation
P.O. Box 16153
Lansing, MI 48901
   This group can supply *Industrial Ventilation: A Manual of Recommended Practice*.

American Lung Association
1740 Broadway
New York, NY 10019
   A good source for information and informative pamphlets. Local chapters in many towns.

Index

Notes

Notes

Notes